JOSEPH KOOT

HIKING EUROPE: MY UPS AND DOWNS

Clifftop
Sackville
New Brunswick
Canada

Second Printing, 2020

Joseph Koot
101 – 15 York Street
Sackville NB
E4L 4R3
Canada

koot.joseph@gmail.com

ISBN 978-0-9936085-4-4

Dedication

With thanks to:

Family and friends for their caring and support

My wife Joanne for her endurance amid my dreams

The folks of Europe for their help during my trek

Acknowledgements

Joanne continued to be supportive in my walking and writing. She kept our extended family and wide group of friends informed of my progress.

I again approached Gerry Bartlett for his suggested improvements in turning the chronicle into a story. Once more, his review of a final draft gave me the confidence to send the book to the printer.

The people of Europe were helpful as I continued my hike. To them I was simply a visitor walking through their lives.

Contents

Foreword

In my book "Europe, One Step at a Time," I told the story of my 6,000-kilometre trek from Portugal to Estonia. The journey required six trips to that continent, and – over six years – I made it from the southwestern to northeastern points of Europe's land mass. That hike had been a healing journey: alone on the trail, I had let my childhood issues find resolution.

Now I returned for a 4,000-kilometre trek in order to complete an "X" through Europe. This would be a hike from the northernmost point of Denmark heading southward and then from the southernmost point of Greece heading northward. "Hiking Europe: My Ups and Downs" is the tale of that struggle.

I passed through a number of European languages, none of which were familiar to me. I have given the highlights of conversations as direct quotations in clear English though they might have been spoken in another language or in more hesitant English.

The narrative in this book is an expansion of the weekly email "Trek Messages" I sent to family and friends back home. On this walk I would use more technology than I had on my first crossing of Europe. Joanne and I used

WhatsApp to send the text of phone messages to each other, and that worked well wherever Internet service was available. I used my iPhone's GPS (Global Positioning System) to direct me along the route, usually clicking on the symbol that showed the walking person that is "hiker GPS," but sometimes opting for the "car GPS."

The back cover of this book shows a "selfie" – taken in Erfurt, Germany – in which I am in discussion with the statue of a lion. This photo reflects my tendency to find solace in the unusual, to stop and review my progress and to see humour in paradoxes. Daily life in foreign cultures provided awkward moments, which are personified in this chat with a lion.

1. Leaving Home

Friday, April 28, 2017

Memories, photos and a self-published book were all that remained of my first trek across Europe. I had begun that hike from Cabo de São Vicente, the southwesternmost point in Portugal back in September of 2007, six months after my retirement at 60 years of age. In hiking I sought to reconcile my childhood as the youngest of a dozen children, my busy married life with five children – and, eventually, eight grandchildren – and my work as a nurse manager in the prison system.

My first hike, starting on September 18, 2007, took me only 176 kilometres before I was assaulted in a park in Aljustrel, Portugal. I returned home bloody and bruised, and I assumed that would be the end of my hiking days. My determination brought me back to the same park the following spring – this time in daylight. The 392 kilometres of that hike took me into Spain and the start of following its pilgrimage routes. A year later my nephew Peter joined me for the first half of my 958 kilometres that completed Spain. The following year I hiked the 988 kilometres from Paris southward to the Spanish border. Then 1,133 kilometres took me through the street where I was born as I covered the distance from Paris to a point just inside Germany. Finally, a gruelling march of 2,371 kilometres deposited me at Estonia's northeastern coast on July 4, 2012.

After one autumn hike and five spring hikes, I had fulfilled a dream of hiking across Europe. I had taken this project seriously, even avoiding ferryboats by going out of my way to cross distant bridges. Out of this pursuit came my publication of two books. "Europe, One Step at a Time" presented the narrative of my experiences as I walked, and it provided insight into my healing as a hiker. The hours spent reviewing my childhood led to my publication of "Looking for Bill, Finding Myself," detailing my birth in the Netherlands, our immigration to Canada and our family life, including my troubled relationship with my brother Bill.

I created a bookmark with an image of the covers of my books. This showed my contact information and would serve as a handout for any European who may be interested in reading about my adventures.

Once again, the project started with placing hiking materials across our guest bed. As the date of departure approached, I removed items to ensure a lighter load. Backpack, T-shirts, shorts, maps, first-aid kit, toiletries and electronics found their place while my hiking boots stood beside the bed as though itching to continue walking.

My paraphernalia were ready, but was I? At 70 years of age, I was now five years older than my age at the end of that first trek. Joanne had been employed at that time, but now she was retired as well. The plan to settle down as a retired couple would be interrupted by my hike. And, of course, we were now on a fixed income, much of which I would use on plane fare, lodging and meals. However, Joanne and I have both said: "You can't ignore your dreams." My completion of the crossing of Europe from west to east called for follow-up with a trek from north to south. Would I reach these goals? Time would tell.

Joanne and I make our way to the Moncton Airport, where our daughter Jessica and family meet us to wish me, "Good luck," on my journey. Two planes full of tourists are preparing for flights to Mexican resorts. It is difficult to squeeze among the potential partygoers and find a place to sit. Then the crowd files down hallways, and the few of us are left to await our flight. An announcement informs us that runway construction in Toronto will postpone our departure by two hours. Passengers spring into action with phone calls to inform others of their delay in arriving at their destination. For my part, I find a comfortable spot away from the conversations and realize I'm already in hiking mode. These absences from home give me the freedom to turn to my inner world for company, and that begins here at Moncton Airport.

Once aboard our Air Canada flight, I'm part of a crowd heading west to go east. We'll be flying west for 1200 kilometres to the hub that is Pearson Airport in Toronto in order to catch a flight east across the Atlantic Ocean to Europe. Only in this recent slice of human history could it make sense to fly westward across one sixth of Canada and recross that path to head eastward toward Europe.

My trip starts toward the end of the Frye Festival taking place in Moncton, New Brunswick. That celebration is billed as Canada's only bilingual international literary festival and the largest literary event in Atlantic Canada, and it brings together authors of all stripes. The festival is named for Northrup Frye who was of humble background, grew up in Moncton and became a world-renowned thinker and literary critic. As it turns out, my seatmate on the flight to Toronto is a fellow author named Wayne Grady. He came to Moncton to serve as panellist at the Frye Festival, and we have a chat about writing.

Wayne suggests: "You may want to read Robert Moor's book, 'On Trails.' He looks at the deeper meaning of following your paths." Apparently, Moor is an American writer who delves into the hiking experience from a philosophical point of view.

At my destination later, I do a search of Wayne Grady's name on my iPhone and realize this seatmate had authored fourteen books of nonfiction, translated over a dozen novels from the French language and edited literary anthologies of fiction and nonfiction. On the plane I saw him as a fellow author; on the ground he leaves me in his dust.

With all the waiting in Moncton, I have little time to connect to my flight to Copenhagen, so my arrival in Toronto requires I go into overdrive. I rush out of the plane, find my gate number on the multi-coloured board and streak down hallways.

As I race down Toronto Airport passageways, I realize how things have changed over the ten years since my first hike in Portugal. Particularly in the area of personal electronics, people are now – frequently and automatically – glancing down at the smart phones in their hands. These gadgets now hold our interactions: they contain everything but our souls. I hike the corridor overlooking another lounge with computer stations set up for easy access to our lives. It is important that all be connected so as to ensure their place in the universe.

At nine o'clock in the evening, I board my Lufthansa flight – operated by Air Canada – to take me to Copenhagen. On my back I carry my little cloth daypack of essentials, and I am once again annoyed with the rolling of suitcases. They block my path, and I'm barred from easy access to my seat. People who would never think of lifting any weight above their heads manage to place these suitcases in overhead bins. They stand back with a look of satisfaction when the whole thing fits. Psychologists might use on-board luggage as a tool to measure a client's trust: "How confident are people in the ability of the complex network that is Air Canada to deliver their suitcases to their destination?"

After all the formalities of flight attendants greeting us on board, teaching us safety procedures and settling people in for a long flight, the giant machine leaves the grasp of earth. Then we become a flying dormitory of grunting and snoring, of crying babies and sprawling bodies. And I realize how much of my hike is about being transported – whether by car, plane, train or bus – to get to my starting points and to return from my end points. Now here I am again, being transported through the air to begin another trek.

Somewhere over the Atlantic, I tune into the 2007 American coming-of-age movie, "Juno," starring two Canadian actors, Ellen Page and Michael Cera. In comparison to those two young people, I feel even older – and certainly less talented. I think about being 70 years old and question the wisdom of hiking almost 2000 kilometres on this trip.

2. Denmark

Saturday, April 29, 2017

The arrival of our flight in Copenhagen is a wake-up call to face passport control, and each of us follows a stranger through a black-ribboned maze toward a sombre official. I survive with no blemish appearing on my electronic travel record. Then I find my way to the flight taking me to Aalborg, Denmark, which lies 100 kilometres short of the starting point of my hike.

This plane is a miniature version of the giant that brought us over the Atlantic. Despite its small size, it's able to take us above a cloud cover and expose us to the sunshine above.

After an uneventful flight, my arrival at the Aalborg airport proves to be a challenge. Other passengers are rewarded with seeing their familiar bags arrive on the conveyor belt. I wait and wait, but my hopes are dashed. As it turns out, my delayed departure from Moncton resulted in a tight connection in Toronto. I made it onto the Copenhagen flight; my backpack did not.

People take their bags and leave the arrivals area. The conveyor belt stops, and I am alone. I see not a single employee.

Sliding glass doors open onto a hallway where a group is lost in conversation. I ask them where to find the office area. They point down a long hall, and I follow it past a series of closed shops to its end. There I find the departure area and, behind a counter, a woman who takes my concerns seriously. Finding a caring person at the end of the airline cobweb is heartwarming.

I knew I would be arriving in Aalborg just after noon on April 29th. I planned to take the bus and train the last 100 kilometres to the town of Skagen, Denmark, lying near the starting point of my trek. There I would spend the night in the Hostelling International facility, which in Denmark is called a "Danhostel." As usual, I have not booked a bed in advance as I was not sure where my air and ground transportation would leave me if I should have a delay in my itinerary.

Now it seems that I will be able to arrive in Skagen this afternoon, so I give the hostel in that town as the destination point for my backpack. The friendly attendant informs me: "We'll send your bag to that hostel by taxi as soon as it gets here on the next flight."

The airport staff do not seem to have reliable information on transportation to Skagen, and I have no Danish SIM card that will let me use my iPhone as I make my way outside the airport. I feel as though I'm stuck at the airport and recall an email message from our daughter: "My pal in Aalborg is Jesper Frank. He's a cool dude. I told him you might be in his neighbourhood."

I had replied: "Perhaps one cool dude will get the chance to meet another!"

I now have the contact information our daughter Laura provided, and the clerk at the airport lets me use her phone to give Jesper a call. He is headed into town to return his son's soccer cleats in exchange for another pair, so he will drop by the airport on his way, he says. Ten minutes later a white BMW drives up, and I hop in.

Jesper is proud of his city of Aalborg and points out the highlights as his son sits quietly in the back seat. Most interesting to me is the fact that the car stalls at each red light; then it starts again when the light turns green. This feature – meant to save on fuel – catches my attention and holds it at each stop. Then I need to remind myself to pay attention to the next bit of his description of Aalborg as the second biggest (after Aarhus), but fastest growing, city of Jutland, the Danish part of the Cimbrian Peninsula.

Jesper is sales representative for a Danish company that provides computer systems used in the publication of newspapers. Our daughter purchased one of these systems for the National Post in Toronto when employed there, and more recently – on two occasions – for The National newspaper in Abu Dhabi.

Jesper, his son and I arrive at a bus station. There we are told that we need the services of a bus depot a block away. The discussion is in Danish and seems to be complex. As it turns out, a problem with a train track requires that I take two buses and a train rather than one bus and one train as would be the normal route. Although many of the Danish service people speak a fair bit of English, I'm pleased that Jesper is there to help me through the muddle.

9

After things are resolved, they leave to buy soccer cleats, following which Jesper and his wife will be attending a wine party at a friend's house. I am left with a handful of tickets and complex instructions: "Wait around the corner for the X-Bus that will take you to the white bus in Frederikshavn. The white bus will bring you to the train in Strandby, and the train will go to your end point at Skagen." I wonder how I might recognize the X-Bus when it pulls up, but I shouldn't have been concerned: on a background of dark blue is a white "X" from top to bottom on each side of the bus. (This is a hopeful omen in my attempt to complete the "X" through Europe.)

In Frederikshavn several of us are waiting for the "white bus," and none of us seems sure what to expect when a yellow and white bus pulls up. That seems to be a local conveyance, and we decide: "That's not our bus." Minutes later the white bus arrives and takes us to the train in Strandby, where we board for the town of Skagen.

A fellow passenger is a post-doctoral engineer from Venice, Italy. He is heading for a phenomenon that occurs at Grenen, the northernmost point of Denmark and the starting point of my trek the next day. At the headland at Grenen, seven kilometres north of Skagen, the Skagerrak Strait from the North Sea and the Kattegat Strait from the Baltic Sea meet. The collision of the waves is often visible as they come from the two straits at an angle to each other. It is this remarkable sight that my fellow passenger came all this way to see. He tells me: "I took only two days off. Then my flight was delayed in Frankfurt, so I had to spend the night there." Now he has only one day left to visit this northern wonder.

The train makes two stops in Skagen. Only at the second stop do I realize that the first stop had been near my hostel. A kilometre and a half of strolling in the evening air, still without luggage, brings me to the hostel. The hosteller greets me in her office, and – to my astonishment – on the floor in a corner sits my backpack. Then she remarks: "I'm glad you're here to claim this bag. I wasn't sure what to do with it when it got here by taxi." I assumed it would take at a day or two to arrive. Instead, it got there before I did!

I am assigned to a 12-bed dormitory in which I am the only occupant, so I have space to organize my backpack for the coming hike. Vehicle license plates in the parking lot showed the letter "N," which I assumed stood for "Netherlands." In fact, that would have been "NL," and the vehicles actually belong to a group from Norway – four adults accompanying a team of 19 boys attending a local soccer camp.

A common occurrence at hostels is the early morning return of partygoers. At 3:00 am someone knocks at the hostel entrance and knocks again. The person may have a legitimate reason to be doing so, perhaps a guest having forgotten the assigned key. I could get up and open the front door but make the wiser choice of staying in bed and drifting off once again.

Sunday, April 30, 2017

Morning light brings the start of this lengthy trek as the next highlight in my post-retirement hiking career. After the usual hearty hostel breakfast offering – cereals, slices of meat and cheese, breads, yogurt and liver paste – I am ready for the day. Now it's time for my seven-kilometre stroll north to locate the starting point of this trek southward across the back of Europe. I leave my backpack at the hostel and take only camera and wallet, so this first day of hiking is a relaxed start to a long journey.

Making my way through the quiet of Sunday morning, I walk streets of cream-coloured stucco houses with bright red roofs. I see no Catholic church and no sign of church attendance among the locals. Town becomes country, with trees and sandy soil but no farms in sight. A terrain of shrubbery turns into dunes with interspersed marram grass. To my surprise, the dunes are populated with a special breed of humans: bird watchers are perched on lawn chairs and have binoculars and cameras at the ready. This community is engaged in getting just the right picture to show fellow bird enthusiasts back home. The area is known to be a major flyway for migrating birds as they return from the south to Greenland and the Scandinavian Peninsula.

Having passed the lighthouse guarding this point, I come upon the tourist shop – with its roof covered in grass – that's central to the beach area called Grenen. On the ground a cement compass, surrounded by a few benches, points toward *Nordstrand*, the north shore, and I continue in that direction. From the Grenen parking lot, tourists are brought to Denmark's most northerly spot by *"Sandormen,"* tractors pulling closed wagons, which look like simple buses.

I escape the crowd's chatter and the tractor's roar to follow my compass to the starting point of my hike. Here I am alone with the water rippling onto the sand as I think of the trek that lies ahead. I take a few selfies and then ask a passerby to snap me in my red T-shirt, long pants and jacket with water lapping at my hiking boots.

I think of the young man I met on the train yesterday and his hope of seeing the offshore phenomenon. Today the sea is so calm that the confluence of the two bodies of water is not even visible – let alone, striking. I feel sorry for him and hope he can come back at another time and stay longer. Across the strait from me, a distant freighter and a sailboat make an interesting scene. I take a photo, but these craft are so far away as to be negligible in the seascape.

I happen upon a nature trail parallel to the shore. It is now quiet and is missing people, birds or activity. Perhaps it will become busier when summer arrives. Along the shore an old German concrete bunker is a reminder of the horrors of war even in such an isolated, peaceful location.

On the way back to the hostel, I stop at a store in Skagen for groceries to serve as my supper. I also get items for tomorrow's breakfast since I shall have a long hike ahead of me, setting out early instead of waiting for the hostel's 8:00 am breakfast. The shop clerk informs me, "There is no phone store in Skagen," so I shall be left without iPhone usage until I reach a town with a bigger commercial area.

With the starting point of my trek behind me, I become reflective and realize that this hike – once again – will have to do with feet, feelings and freedom. My feet will need to keep moving, bringing out feelings that normally lie buried while I get a sense of freedom despite the limitations of the trail.

In the quiet Sunday afternoon, I sprawl on the hostel lobby couch and dose off. I use the microwave oven to heat up the slices of pizza I bought earlier and enjoy an early supper. Some of the birders are fellow guests at the hostel, and they arrive back exuberant about today's successful sightings.

I get out my hiking poles and extend them to their proper length. Then I repack in preparation for tomorrow's vigorous hike. Finally I do a bit of darning – mending a loop on my cloth daypack that holds two strings in place.

As I drift off for the night, I recognize my earworm: "There's no shore like the north shore. That's for shore." This is the catchphrase of "Lucien," a character our Moncton comedian, Marshall Button, developed from his experiences working in the paper mill in his hometown of Dalhousie on New Brunswick's north shore. And I think of home and fall asleep.

Monday, May 1, 2017

I have a long day's hike ahead of me, so I'm pleased to arise at 5:00 am. I munch on the breakfast items I bought yesterday (crackers, sliced meat and yogurt) and get on my way by 5:50 when it is already light in this northerly location. As I leave the hostel and hike out of Skagen and into the country, I'm buffeted by gusts from the east.

My path is taking me southward on the Cimbrian Peninsula whose northern tip I visited yesterday. I'll be hiking that peninsula for 500 kilometres until I near Hamburg in northern Germany. As I get further from the tip, I continue to see dunes beyond scraggly pine trees to my left. Then a few signs of farm activity appear, including a horse barn with some of the animals outside for exercise. And I realize that I'll spend the next two months out for exercise. Eventually I'll once again feel as though my body is turning into a machine. However, that will take days, and in the meantime walking is simply hard work.

At home before this trek, I printed a copy of the GPS (Global Positioning System) trail from my computer. I typed "Skagen, Denmark to Ljubljana, Slovenia," clicked on the walking person image and received a suggested hiking trail. We have hope in technology; we trust technology. I was sure that my printed instructions of turning left, turning right or going straight ahead would be useful. However, I now realize two things: the instructions mention street names that do not always appear on signposts when I need them, and the route does not take me past the hostel in the next town, the point where I am headed for the night. Within hours the bundle of pages becomes useless; within days I convince myself to assign this path in life to the nearest garbage can, unfortunately.

As usual, my first day gives hints of what may cause problems on my path. For unknown reasons, a toenail is feeling irritated and a tendon in my foot is making itself felt. This may or may not be a warning of future issues. Meanwhile I'll just have to hope these things resolve while a short passenger train speeds into the distance. Though I envy those who can sit on that train and be transported, I remind myself that this continuous trek is my own choice.

The highway alternates between two and three lanes, providing points where cars can overtake and pass each other. It's an attractive road with a well-tended grass shoulder, which thankfully leads to my first bicycle path of the trek. Beside the road a series of anthills appears and is backed by a continuous row of pine trees. Beyond the trees lie campgrounds, and the odd small farm between the scruffy dunes.

I pass an *"automat"* – a gas station with no one in attendance. The gasoline is priced at 10.26 DKK, and diesel at 8.49 DKK. I'm being exposed to another system of currency with the Danish *krone* (contracted to DKK, and *kroner* in its plural form). I struggle with fathoming how the value of the *krone* compares to the Canadian dollar or to the Euro of the European Union. These mathematical puzzles can be challenging.

A lasting memory of my hike through Europe will be the number of times I arrive at businesses that are closed. Now I hike 25 kilometres before I arrive at a cup of coffee in the village of Jerup as other shops have been closed because it is Monday. And my confusion over "which businesses are open when" continues.

The last eight kilometres of the day are tough, and I finally slide into the city of Frederikshavn. Without a Danish SIM card in my iPhone, I still don't have access to the Internet and cannot ascertain the whereabouts of the hostel where I'll spend the night. I ask three different people who help me pinpoint its location.

The Danhostel manager is a friendly chap, and I complete the application for a Hostelling International membership card, which gives me a discount on my stays. We get into a discussion on the area's history, and the hosteller is especially proud of one statistic: "During the war, Denmark saved the lives of 90% of its Jewish people. They sent them to Sweden on ships."

The fellow recognizes my fatigue and assigns me my own room for the night, one with four bunk beds. Settled in my quarters, I look back on my day and think of a comment to share with Joanne. We have given one of our friends back home in Sackville handfuls of the sweet woodruff serving as ground cover in our side garden. This woman is a German immigrant and follows their custom of flavouring white wine with a few sprigs of the herb when it is in flower. Now I use the hostel Wi-Fi to send Joanne a text message: "Today I saw a large patch of woodruff in flower. Too bad I had no wine with me!"

I find a little restaurant for supper although my stomach is starting to do flips as it has so often during the first few days of each hike. I order a plate of spaghetti and rush to the toilet, making it in time to empty my stomach into the bowl. After washing up and rinsing my mouth, I return to my table ready to tackle my meal.

I feel exhausted after this 40-kilometre day that took me to the first hostel after Skagen. On the good side, such a long hike forces out the kinks that have built up since the last trek. And it will make other days seem short.

On my past trips, I had worn sandals in the evenings, but my sensitivity to their plastic features made that footwear irritating. This time I had brought my bedroom slippers – footwear that is light and can be squeezed into my backpack. Now I stroll around Frederikshavn's downtown in my slippers and try to ascertain where I can buy a SIM card for my phone in the morning.

Tuesday, May 2, 2017

From previous experience I know that obtaining a SIM card can take some time, so I decide to "take the day off." However, I'm up at 6:00 o'clock and outside to enjoy the stillness of dawn. The hostel proves to be modern and relaxed, and breakfast is served in an area with windows exposing us to morning light.

To meet my goal for the day, I head to a phone store when businesses open. As it turns out, the clerk tells me: "To sell you a SIM card, we need to see identification. That has to be the yellow CPI card."

I'm confused: "What's a yellow CPI card?"

"It's the Danish health certificate. Don't you have one?"

"No. I'm visiting from Canada. Could you use my passport instead?"

"No. It has to be the health certificate." So, I leave its doors frustrated with having no SIM card.

It is suggested I purchase a Lycamobile SIM card at the Fakta grocery store, so I get one there. However, the helpful Fakta employee adds: "Our SIM card only has phone minutes but not data. Try the 'You See' store around the corner to see if they can add the data. If they can't, then just return the SIM card here, and we'll give your money back."

I take a break from the hunt and return to the hostel. The hosteller is astonished that I couldn't get a SIM card at the phone store without a government health card. I make my way to "You See," but I have a problem recalling my new password, which I left at the hostel. So, I go back to the hostel to get the password information for the SIM card I had bought at the Fakta grocery store. When I get back to "You See," they clarify: "We can only provide minutes but not data. Try the Fotex department store. It uses a different company's SIM card that includes data."

I hope to be close to ending my search and simply having to go back to the Fakta grocery store. There I'll return its SIM card and go to Fotex to get a new one – the one with both minutes and data. For being only a centimetre square, this little phone device is costing me an inordinate amount of time and irritation.

Bible stories speak of angels appearing in order to assist lonely travellers in their journeys. In my case, Alexander is such an angel. As the electronics clerk in the Fotex store, he explains the process, inserts the SIM card and sends me on my way. It takes only a minute or two and is followed by my sigh of relief.

Armed with an iPhone with data, I pay a visit to the tourism office to learn a little more about this attractive little city with its central street used only for pedestrian traffic. Then, still wearing my slippers and with no one complaining about it, I stop at the outdoor patio of the quaintly named "2takt Cafe & Brasserie" for a mug of hot chocolate just as the sun appears from behind cloud cover. This is a hopeful omen. However, after all my work, Joanne has trouble contacting me at my new phone number. We finally sort things out and have a little chat, and the sun keeps shining.

During the night a strange dream indicates that I must be feeling the pressure to keep walking. In that fantasy I am visiting my sister, and she suggests: "Take a look at the greenhouse we built in the garage," (whatever a greenhouse in a garage might be!). I reply that I'll look later, but then realize I need to look immediately as I'll have to keep walking in the morning.

Wednesday, May 3, 2017

I arise at 5:10, and I'm hiking by 6:15. It always takes about an hour to dress, have breakfast and repack before heading out. No matter how I try to shorten that period, it doesn't work: it takes time to squeeze my possessions into the backpack in such a way as to have easy access to things I might need on the trail.

Today there is only a slight breeze from the north. It's starting to feel like summer, and I look forward to wearing my shorts. So far in Denmark, I have only had to walk on the shoulder of the road for about 10 kilometres. Now I'm delighted that the road I'm following leads to another bike path. With their limited bicycle traffic and level surfaces, these paved stretches allow for a comfortable hike. Occasionally other slow vehicles use these paths: in one case, that is a miniature truck – with a big man driving and with one wheel in the front and two in the back – crawling along at about 10 kilometres per hour. I find the whole picture amusing.

At the roomy restaurant of a truck stop, I am the only customer as I enjoy a coffee. It's still early in the season, and it will likely be busier in a month or so. A few kilometres along, I pass groups of houses as well as unhurried campgrounds, hotels and eateries.

Just past a series of pig farms, I spot a roadside picnic table where I snack on *chilepostej* (chili-flavoured liver paste) on sesame seed crackers, as well as a drink of blackberry yogurt. In this little park, I recognize the lesson the trees around me are teaching. Their leaves show I've gone through several spring seasons: back home the leaves were being born after winter's cold; around Toronto Airport they were juveniles; here they are reaching summer's glory.

As the road veers away from the coast, the surroundings become farm country – cattle, crops, potatoes and horses – with not a hostel (or a cup of coffee) in sight. In such a rural area, I would normally welcome nature's aromas. To my disappointment, the pervasive smell is one of chemicals that have been sprayed onto the fields.

My iPhone shows few sizable towns in the area, and I grow concerned about finding a bed for the night. In a village a woman is busy in her yard, and I ask about a hotel. Her simple answer is, "Hjallerup." That town is some distance away, and I realize this may be another long day.

With technology comes the availability of distant resources, so I send Joanne a text message to seek her advice. I assume she could take some time to research what might be available in my area – time that I don't have with my need to keep walking. As it turns out, Joanne doesn't reply as she is busy with one of the activities that continue at home while I'm hiking through Europe. When she does respond, she checks Google Earth to help guide me to my destination, and the discussion goes like this.

Joseph: "I'm looking for a hotel for the night about 30 kilometres north of Aalborg. Any suggestions?" "I'm on Route 180." "Now headed for the hotel in Hjallerup."

Joanne: "Oh sorry. Just got home. Didn't see message. Did you make it to hotel?"

Joseph: "Almost!"

Joanne: "Did you get to the industrial section yet?" "Where you have to turn right?"

Joseph: "It's coming up." "First industry is on my left."

Joanne: "Need help or are you ok?"

Joseph: "Left at lights, then right. I see it."

Joanne: "Ok talk later!"

An hour later I text:

"Had a hot shower. Now at supper." "That was 44 km today. Not planned. A few touristy hotels early in the day, but only farmland later. Not a coffee to be had!"

Another hour and a half later, Joanne texts:

"Just got home from crocheting class . . ."

So, after a 44-kilometre day, I fall into a hotel in Hjallerup. This is an older hotel, part of which has seen renovation. It is a tidy place and, at 86 Euros, expensive as are so many of the food and lodging services in Denmark.

This hotel has salmon steak dinner on the menu, and my nauseated stomach only allows me to eat half of it. My tummy keeps reminding me that I have to find a way to limit my hiking to 30 kilometres a day.

I go to bed exhausted.

Thursday, May 4, 2017

Arising at 6:30, I take my time enjoying the breakfast provided by the hotel as I'm not in a hurry with only 20 kilometres ahead of me today. I seem to have recuperated from yesterday's fatigue, and I'm buffeted by cool gusts from the north as I pass fertile, well-tended farms that specialize in cash crops. I pass a horse riding school where the animals are outside and walking around in a circular pen while a machine pushes a piece of canvas behind each horse to keep it moving. I prefer my own motivation and a more interesting path.

I stop for coffee at a bakery in the village of Vodskov. Upon leaving, I realize I'm nearing Aalborg as a plane ascends from a runway. The bicycle path I'm using curves beside a highway busy with traffic where a sign indicates that Aalborg is only four minutes away. I realize the information is not meant for me when another sign shows a speed limit of 110 kilometres per hour! As I crawl along, I'm destined for those four minutes to become an hour and a half before I enter the city.

I'm excited to see a McDonald's outlet ahead of me and look forward to a coffee and a well-earned hot fudge sundae. As I approach, I notice the parking lot has several commercial vans and no other customers. Unfortunately, the place is closed for renovation with an anthill of workers measuring, sawing and hammering.

My fear of crossing high bridges seems to be coming under control, as the bridge into Aalborg causes me little anxiety. At its other end, a small ship is anchored, and – to my delight – its hull reads, *"Prinses Juliana"* (princess Juliana) and a sign says "Restaurant, Amsterdam." This is a floating restaurant and it would be nice to have some *poffertjes* (miniature pancakes), a fresh herring or a croquette. As I approach, I realize that the white tablecloths and the array of silverware and stemmed glasses are not what I had in mind. So, I keep walking.

As I approached this city, I saw colourful posters announcing the circus. Now, in a park area, three elephants are loitering next to some carnival tents. I take a few pictures and continue on my way.

I understand the hostel to be near the north end where I entered the city. In fact, it is another hour of walking (about five kilometres) westward to the edge of the built-up area. I keep watching for the telltale symbol of Hostelling International (HI), a blue triangle holding a white house and tree. As it turns out, the hostel recently switched from being part of the HI family, so it does not display that symbol. As a result, I pass the lane where it is located, turn back and finally find my bed for the night. Today I anticipated a 20-kilometre hike, but that has become at least 25 kilometres.

The hostel lacks the comfortable atmosphere I enjoy. Instead, this is a seminar facility with cabins for participants. On the good side, it has computer terminals (though challenging me with its Danish keyboard), so I can type my "Trek Message 1" to family and friends back home. On the bad side, after four hours in the clothes dryer, my laundry is still too damp to pack. If the cause of this is an energy-saving feature, it doesn't work as I restart the dryer over and over. This keeps me from retiring till much past my bedtime. I finally crank up the hot water register in my room and spread my damp clothes on it so things will be toasty by morning.

Upon my arrival in Denmark, I was helped by Jesper Frank from here in Aalborg. So, before settling in for the night, I send him an e-mail message: "I've hiked to Aalborg, and I'm staying in a hostel here overnight. I'll continue southward early tomorrow morning. Thanks, again, for your help with the train and bus confusion. I had no trouble with the trip, and my backpack had already arrived in Skagen by taxi."

Jesper replies: "You are more than welcome. (Our surprise party went well and lasted till 2 in the morning.) You should have great weather the next couple of days, so hopefully you will enjoy Denmark ;-) Good luck and all the best. Feel free to call should you run into any issues." And so, I leave another helpful person behind in my unending trek.

Friday, May 5, 2017

In the early morning, I pack my freshly laundered clothes. After a breakfast of leftover liver paste on crackers, the last of a bottle of yogurt and an orange, I'm on my way. On a bicycle path, I pass a metre-high square metal unit that looks like a black post with a hose hanging from it. On the front it has the word *"Luft"* (air) and turns out to be a tire pump for passing cyclists. And I'm reminded that a bike would have made my trek quicker as I trudge along.

This is an area of long slopes, with the sidewalk going up or down for a great distance. I stop at a grocery store for a coffee and then spy a McDonald's for a chocolate ice cream sundae. Later for lunch I find a cafeteria where I enjoy a sandwich with a mixture of sliced meats, European style.

I'm making my way into farm country, with one field of canola in bloom covering about 100 acres. Communities form a neat pattern of productive farms interspersed with tidy towns. As I pass a *planteskole* (literally, "plant school," a tree nursery), I'm amused at the words used in various languages to indicate that these trees and shrubs are still in their formative stage of attending school.

Following a 26-kilometre hike, I arrive in the town of Rebild where the hostel, unfortunately, has no vacancy. The woman in reception suggests: "An older couple have a bed and breakfast nearby. I'll give you the address." The elderly man and woman become my hosts for the night. These folks have made two rooms available for guests by storing their worldly possessions behind drapes that block off sections of the ground floor. Their life stories must be piled behind those curtains.

There would have been no vacancy here, but a guest from France had taken a flight home because of illness in the family. I have mixed emotions: I feel bad about this unknown person's plight while happy with not having to look further for a room. Tommy, a fellow guest from Norway, is attending a course in jewellery design in the area. He comments: "Rebild has a lot of places for tourists to stay, but many of those are full. It already gets busy here in the spring."

Before settling in for the night, I walk the two blocks to the Danhostel where there had been no room earlier. I ask the receptionist: "Can you book a room for me at the Danhostel in Hobro? I'll be staying there tomorrow night." Moments later she has reserved a room through their system, and I'm free of worry about this part of Denmark being so busy that I'll not find a bed in Hobro.

Saturday, May 6, 2017

I have asked my host couple for an early breakfast, and now I dine alone at a well-worn table covered with an orange cloth. By 8:00 am I'm out the door and into the country.

After days of rolling landscape, I've now entered an area of rounded deciduous trees covering rounded hills. A young Polish couple get off their bikes ahead of me, and I ask them what is so attractive in the area. They are exuberant with details: "It's just like a park here, and we enjoy the trees and hills and flocks of sheep."

They tell me that others arrive to take in the American connection to this area. Local people who had immigrated to the USA had provided funding to establish the Rebild National Park. Each July 4th crowds arrive to celebrate American Independence Day and take pictures of the bronze relief of Abraham Lincoln.

Leaving the park, I climb an unending hill with forest all around. This must be an introduction to the mountains I can expect in Austria. I take off my jacket and wonder when it will be time to don my shorts. Further along, at a white hotel in Rold, I am served coffee on the terrace. A few other men arrive as they wait for their wives who are busy with a dress sale at a store across the street.

I'm starting to recognize repetitive signs, such as *"Til Salg"* (for sale), which appears in front of some houses. I have seen many homes for sale and imagine buying one and surprising Joanne with our move to Denmark. It seems a pleasant land, and our European background would help us adjust. But no, I just keep on walking.

Further along, a modern structure of glass and wood proves to be a market with a busy ice cream stand. I consider joining the long line of customers but notice that this is not real ice cream but fluffed concoction out of a machine. I don't want to stand and wait for something that may not be to my liking, so I hike out of there.

At the end of 35 kilometres, I arrive in the town of Hobro and pass a Volkswagen dealership with windows serving as its walls. It would be interesting to see how this agency compares to those back home, so I hike to its front doors. However, the notice of *Åbningstider* (opening hours) on the door includes, *"Lørdag lukket"* (Saturday closed). I'm astonished that a car dealership would not be available for sales on Saturday, a time when most people would be off work and free to buy a new vehicle. I'll chalk it up to another European mystery.

I continue to the far end of town where I locate the hostel that had been booked for me by the hosteller in Rebild. A number of families are setting up a group barbecue in the side yard, but I don't get invited.

In some ways this hike feels like my previous ones – simply a constant trek. In other ways, there are differences. I've been more successful in going from one hostel to another over the period of a day. I also have a few new pieces of gear – two water containers that were a birthday present from our daughter Rebecca's family, two T-shirts to replace my old faded ones, as well as new boots, hat and rain poncho. This time I have the convenience of an iPhone to help me locate hostels. And, of course, I'm now 70 and was 10 years younger at the start of my first hike across Europe. Thankfully, my fear of high bridges seems to be lessening. But, again on this trek, my stomach has been problematic although it is now settling as shown in these text messages.

Joanne: "Next place is Randers I think maybe? But is 33km by car and they show the big highway!" "What's for supper for you tonight?"

Joseph: "Randers is my destination tomorrow. I found an oriental restaurant because I hadn't had soup since leaving home. Soup, spring rolls and jasmine tea. It settled my stomach."

Joanne: "Oh good! Did the ice cream at Mickey D do that yesterday?"

Joseph: "Sure did!"

Joanne: "I thought so. Ice cream every day will make the tummy ache go away!"

Sunday, May 7, 2017

There must be a car show somewhere as older models pass from time to time, including the odd Ford and Chevrolet from the 1950's. I've seen more classic cars on the roads here than I normally see in Canada – or in other countries, for that matter.

Yard work must be a Sunday priority as I see many cars pulling utility trailers. Some of these hold lawn mowers; others are piled with branches going to a landfill.

During the first part of Denmark, about half of my hike took place on bicycle paths. Recently I've been disappointed with the lack of bike trails, and I spend most of my time on the shoulders of roads, sharing space with passing cars. I've tried to understand which communities give bicycles their own routes and which do not. Their presence or absence seems to have little to do with the layout of the terrain, the number of people or the distance from towns. Perhaps construction of bike paths is simply the result of a local politician's preferences.

After 28 kilometres I get to the city of Randers and find the sidestreet where the hostel is located. My iPhone map brings me to a cluttered mansion that seems to be deserted. I can't imagine sleeping here tonight, and no one answers my knock, so I look around for someone to ask about this place. I notice a row of trees across the road and enter a lane; and there I find my hostel, which is a great improvement over the deserted mansion.

This facility is unstaffed, but a speaker system outside the door connects me to someone back in Aalborg. The disembodied voice, from the hostel where I had stayed in Aalborg, gives me the code to open the door and explains which room will be mine for the night. As was the case in Aalborg, this hostel is not part of the Hostelling International (HI) system and doesn't have the friendly atmosphere that comes with HI designation. Instead, this is only a building, though fulfilling my priorities of bed, shower and breakfast.

I'm alone in this four-storey structure till a group of enthusiastic football (i.e. soccer) players from Manchester, England arrives back from their sports event. They are taking part in a competition with local teams, and I strain to understand their dialect as they ask about Canada. I didn't believe a recent news item, which stated that soon people in North America and England would no longer understand each other's English. It was mentioned that the languages were drifting apart, with each area's dialect becoming more and more distinct. After failing to decipher another question from these Mancunians, I give up and realize that, linguistically, we have already gone our separate ways.

As on previous trips, parts of my body are taking turns in providing aches and pains. My stomach seems to have settled, but now the little toe of my left foot is asking for attention.

Monday, May 8, 2017

This hostel seemed impersonal when I arrived – having to talk to a human voice through a speaker system. However, this morning's extensive, tasty breakfast is provided by a chatty woman. I ask her: "Do you have time to come outside and take my picture?" We choose the board fence in the side yard as background, and I pose in long pants and jacket in the coolness of early morning. This photo will be added to the few from each hike that serve as confirmation of where I've been.

On the way out of Randers, I stop at a bank to ask for directions. To my surprise, the place consists of eight people standing at computer desks along the wall. The man who answers my inquiries is helpful, and he laughs at my question: "If this is a bank, where's all the money?"

He says they have none, and I reply: "This is Denmark. I'm sure you have lots of money!" In fact, I've heard it said that the economy is making a real comeback here, and support services for business people (such as hotels) are busy.

From time to time, I see art installations in unusual places, and here in Randers I pass a two-storey red-brick apartment building, which features five planks set on the ground leaning against one end wall. Each board is painted a bright colour – purple, black, yellow, dark blue and light blue –

and their ends almost reach the roof. In another part of this same housing area, a white structure looks like a simple apartment building with four tiers of windows. However, it is not really a building – just an empty shell serving as an art form to communicate ideas. Europe's works of art often sneak up on me, and they provide a pleasant diversion.

As in my past hikes in Europe, the McDonald's outlets continue to make an impression. In my solitary hike through the isolation of countryside or the aloofness of towns, McDonald's provides familiarity. I can count on their coffee to be fresh, their service to be friendly and their washrooms to be clean.

In pondering my wish for some consistency in the uncertainties of my hikes across Europe, I compare my life on the trail with a settled life at home. People find comfort in family recipes, a favourite armchair or a familiar piece of music. Such things provide a waymark as we humans tumble through space and time. McDonald's provides me with consistency as I hike through space and time.

And so it is that, at the edge of town, I see the McDonald's arches off in the distance. Only their top parts are visible but so small as to be part of the neon landscape. However, these bits of golden arches are meaningful enough – perhaps, in my subconscious – that I salivate and set course to a coffee and chocolate sundae. The interior of this outlet is of the standard McDonald's variety, but here two wooden stepstools, bright with splashes of paint, are intended so that younger customers can see above the counter. It's a thoughtful touch.

On the 38-kilometre hike into the city of Aarhus, I am pushed along by a cold gale from the northeast as I head southward and meet examples of the old and the new – a farmstead with thatched roof on house and barn; an egg-shaped bus shelter looking like something out of the future.

At some point two major roads come together, and I need to cross a bridge over a four-lane highway streaming with traffic. I expect the usual discomfort that comes from all that movement at the edge of my field of vision, but it does not happen. Instead, I calmly walk across.

Entering the sprawling city of Aarhus, I pass a giant IKEA store where I ask a young couple: "Do you know the way to the hostel? My iPhone doesn't show this new road, so I'm confused." Their names are Maia and Tony, and they are pushing a baby carriage holding little Fia. They explain the route I should take and then ask about my hike, which they find fascinating. I hand them a bookmark showing the covers of three of my books and indicating where the books are available. They have a few more questions about my trek and plan to find my books on Amazon.

I follow their instructions to follow the main road and take a left turn on the interestingly named street, *Nordvestpassagen* (Northwest Passage). From there I follow a complex, twisted route to the Aarhus hostel. This friendly building is located in a "forest" (as the hosteller calls it) with deciduous trees spreading in all directions.

I celebrate my arrival with some nachos and a small dark beer at "Ziggy's," a bar where I use their Wi-Fi service to have my first WhatsApp back-and-forth chat with Joanne. After sorting out how to get WhatsApp to access the microphone in "Settings," Joanne and I send each other little bits of conversation on how we are doing and, particularly, the condition of my stomach. I assure Joanne that it has now settled as I feast on nachos and beer, and I send her a video of my plate with the buzz of the after-work bar crowd in the background.

Tuesday, May 9, 2017

There are close to 100 children at the hostel, all having breakfast at once. I escape to the quiet of my trek, which takes me through downtown Aarhus with its orderly buildings, winding canal and relaxed crowds. I've followed Route 180 since Frederikshavn and need to find Route 170 as it heads southward. With luck and intuition, I chance upon a street that takes me in the right direction, and I'm on my way out of the city.

For the first time on this trek, it starts to rain, and I try out my new bright red rain poncho. I had bought my former poncho in a shop at the start of the Spanish Camino in May of 2009. It had taken me through many storms but had stopped being waterproof. Before leaving home, I had not been able to find a replacement locally but – through the wonders of the Internet – ordered a similar item from India, of all places. It arrived within days and should now serve me well.

For a break from the weather, I stop at a little restaurant for a pot of green tea and a serving of pickled herring, which comes with capers, curry sauce, salad and slices of thickly buttered rye bread. That fortifies me for the journey.

Today's 27 kilometres takes me over a series of hills and past a lake to a hostel of cabins, canoes and teenagers at the edge of the town of Skanderborg. In the Hostelling International chain in Denmark, each Danhostel is pleasant, clean and armed with a generous breakfast as is this facility. The cabin that serves as my home for the night is next to that of four boys who ask me the odd question: "Where do you come from? Where are you going?" Theirs is the noisiest hut with shouts and laughter, but they soon settle down for the evening.

The Mylar lining of my rain poncho has become a trap for perspiration, so both the inside and outside of the material are wet. I drape it over a chair near the window so it will be dry by morning. Then I wash T-shirt, socks and underwear in the sink and hang these items in strategic places around the rain poncho, turning my hostel room – once again – into a mini-laundromat. Then I retire for the night in this bucolic setting.

Wednesday, May 10, 2017

Leaving the hostel, I guess at my path and, fortunately, find myself back on Route 170 as it runs alongside a major four-lane highway (as Route 180 had done). The GPS on my iPhone has been useful, but it doesn't always provide detail on the way out of towns. Then I rely on my trusty compass, traffic patterns and distant views to lead me back into rural areas.

Today is forecast to be wet. Having rain start and stop is an irritation for a hiker. It requires putting on and taking off the poncho over and over in order to stay dry while not perspiring excessively. Today this is not the case: it rains constantly, all day long.

Joanne sends me a few text messages about the road *(vej)* I am taking: "It looks like you are in a busier area. Are you on 170 now? On the Skanderborgvej?" "Are you on the Hovedvejen yet? Nice places to walk through. I think you will find some coffee on your walks today!"

Small farms with sheep and horses (including a man practising his sulky racing) are interspersed with factories.

34

Sometimes a few curious cows approach a fence as I pass, and I'm tempted to take them along on my trek. Further north, there had been many houses with *"Til Salg"* (for sale) signs. Now those signs are more likely to be advertising an empty industrial building, and few houses are looking for new owners.

Entering the city of Horsens, I pass a hotel that is all glass and soaring wooden pillars, so I drop in to take a look. Small groups of business people come and go while I have a chat with the staff. They assure me that, from their point of view, the economy is doing well.

Then I turn down a few side streets and, at the end of today's 24-kilometre hike, I arrive at the hostel – a fancy place with only three men as guests. Hostels now rarely have computers available since most visitors have smart phones, so I go in search of the city library where I type my "Trek Message 2" to family and friends. My MacBook Pro back home is painless compared to the challenges I face in dealing with the library's Danish keyboard.

Thursday, May 11, 2017

In the morning I leave the quiet hostel in a warm drizzle and have someone take a picture of me in my unflattering rain poncho. As I leave, I realize I am now at the point of hiking more automatically – as though I have switched into second gear.

On the way out of Horsens, I stop at a bakery to make sure the street I am following does, in fact, lead to the highway. I am met with enthusiasm by the bakery owner: "Here's a cup of coffee and a cinnamon roll. I'd like a newspaper reporter to come and talk to you. Is that okay?" She asks me to stay while she phones the local newspaper, the *Horsens Folkeblad*, to have them cover my story.

Ten minutes later Ingeborg enters the bakery with a full smile, shoulder-length dark hair and a notepad at the ready. We have an hour-long chat, during which she needs to search for the odd English word but is enthusiastic about my adventures since starting in Portugal ten years ago. Outside the bakery she takes a few photos and a video of my hiking.

That afternoon Ingeborg sends an email message with a link to the article. I click on it to see a few pictures and a write-up in Danish. Back home Joanne asks our neighbour Lizzi Hansen, a woman of Danish background, to translate the item for us. Her version of the first paragraph is as follows: "Joseph Koot stuck his head in at the Lagkagehuset ['Layer Cake House,' the bakery] on Sønderbrogade in Horsens. He asks direction to Vejle, a distance to be covered on foot, mind you! The 70-year-old Canadian is on a trek through most of Europe. After a bed for the night and a solid breakfast at the hostel in Horsens, he is ready for Thursday's hike from Horsens to Vejle." The interview creates more memories to join the many I've formed throughout Europe.

Soon the sun comes out although it proves to be a long hike to Vejle – feeling longer because of the distraction of the press coverage that started my day. Nearing the town of Vejle, I rest on a bench in a roadside park. The park is equipped with a gadget that looks like the horn of a trumpet. It runs down to a garbage can, and cars slow down to dispose of their trash in this trumpet and then continue on their way.

I have assumed the hostel would be within the town, but it takes me an hour and a half to hike another seven kilometres into the country, for a total of 35 kilometres today.

At my destination I find the hostel locked, but a phone on the outside wall and instructions in several languages advise me to call the manager. She arrives within minutes.

This woman is friendly but stern: "We have such nice trails here. You should hike on those, not along the road." She offers me a detailed map but can't advise me on how to cross the river a kilometre or two from here. I decide to stick to Denmark's roads as I'm sure they come designed with bridges.

Friday, May 12, 2017

At the hostel a simple breakfast of bread with cheese and meat, as well as sliced fruit and yogurt, is provided for me as the only guest. The cheese slicer is a combination of technology and art: you turn a handle, which holds a wire that slices the square piece of cheese on its board. The corkscrew axis takes the handle downward to the next slice. This is truly a breakfast novelty.

Today is the Danish holy day, *Store Bededag*. Also known as Great Prayer Day, or General Prayer Day, this is a special Danish festival celebrated on the fourth Friday after Easter Sunday. It is a collection of minor Christian holy days consolidated into one. I was informed, "Everything will be closed." However, with so few commercial establishments in towns on my way, I don't notice much difference.

I stop to take a look at the interior of a church. It is a simple country chapel of white stucco and little ornamentation where families are gathering for a service. Each arrival is marked by chatter, hugs and handshakes all around as the pews begin to fill. The adjacent cemetery has rows of hedges separating the burial plots from each other. It is a peaceful spot.

A series of small roads takes me through rolling terrain to Route 176. A brisk wind from the east caresses my left shoulder as I clear a hill. Then, in the next valley, it is calm and pleasant.

As I near the city of Kolding after 28 kilometres, I hope for a bike path along the busier roads, but no such convenience appears. I find the hostel near the entrance to town and directly in line with the next town. I'm always pleased when the path to and from the hostel is in line with my southerly direction. It can be frustrating to detour away from my intended route toward a distant hostel.

As a change from our normal text messages, Joanne and I set up a FaceTime conversation. It will be fun to see each other in person and to connect once again.

Joseph: "I'm now in Kolding. Just arrived at hostel. Need shower and some supper. What time do you want to call? Would Face Time or something work, or just phone. Whichever you prefer."

Joanne: "Let's try FaceTime when you are finished your supper. I'm here."

Joseph: "How about two hours from now. I'll WhatsApp when I'm ready."

Joanne: "Ok sounds good!"

Joseph (two hours later): "I'm ready. What do I need to do for the call?"

Joanne: "I'll call you." Over the vast distance and across an ocean, technology connects us once again.

I continue to be disappointed that some European countries do not serve soup in summer. It is one "food group" that my stomach finds soothing. Instead, I take a path through the hostel garden and down a hill to a food stand with the biggest pita kebab I've ever seen. It proves to be a meal so large I can't finish it.

Later Joanne and I have an electronic "discussion," using WhatsApp. We speak a sentence or two into the iPhone microphone, send that message, listen to the reply from the other end and send the response – all this over thousands of kilometres. The topic of our discussion is not momentous: it concerns how to reset the time on one of our bedside clocks by placing the iPhone on the clock's port. So, not earth shattering.

Saturday, May 13, 2017

My home for the night in Kolding proves to be the nicest hostel I've ever seen and the least expensive one in Denmark so far. The lobby and eating area are open, airy and bright. The rooms are spotless, with three fluorescent squares of glass above the bed in my private room serving as subdued lighting and giving the room a space-age appearance. The bathrooms smell fresh and are armed with efficient showers.

Breakfast consists of the usual variety of breads, meats, cheeses, fruit and yogurt. However, here we also have a choice of freshly made waffles, and they are delicious. I appreciate the efficient actions of the woman who owns the place and of the young man, in his serious green apron, who is kept moving as he brings out fresh food from the kitchen. Large windows let in the morning sun and highlight the bottles of wine for sale, serving as decoration in the dining area, while small oil paintings decorate the walls and add a touch of colour. I regret leaving this haven as I take the stairs down the hill into the centre of Kolding. This will lead me out into the country and to my next destination.

A church is open as I leave town, and I enter for a glance at this serious house of prayer. Our Catholic churches in Europe tend to be decorative and uplifting in their statues of saints, stained glass and priest's vestments. Protestant churches are sombre and simple. In this church the minister is preaching from a pulpit of dark wood while dressed in black cassock with white ruffled collar. The Catholic church atmosphere seems uplifting; the Protestant one feels stern. Most pews are full, but people near the entrance appear more interested in my hiker's look than in the sermon, so I leave quietly.

On a downtown side street, a Saturday morning market is setting up with stalls of vegetables and other merchandise. I approach a woman selling potted plants and ask her where I'd find an *apotek* (pharmacy). It is a block or two away, and there I buy a box of bandage material. I will be able to cut off a piece at a time to protect my latest blisters.

In Europe the pharmacy staff are kept busy giving health advice while in Canada their work consists of giving instructions on taking the medication prescribed by the doctor. I ask the pharmacist about the dry area under my lower lip, and she advises: "It's not eczema. I think it's from too much sun and wind." I decide to apply my daytime sunscreen and nighttime Vaseline more diligently.

To balance out my series of positive experiences in Kolding, I am faced with a negative: four big black dogs snarl and bark at me from behind a rickety fence. A white pooch with black spots is running between them, yelping as though wanting to be in on the action. I still don't understand the need to own a bunch of such beasts.

Along a lonely stretch of road, I stop at a picnic table for a snack when a cherry-red 1975 Pontiac Grand Ville convertible pulls up. The middle-aged couple are on their way to a demonstration of classic cars in the town of Haderslev, where I am headed for the night. Each of us has a pursuit, and they speed away with the car's top down and with hair flying while I crawl along.

Kilometres further, Kro hotel staff have only a few minutes to bring me a cup of coffee. They are overwhelmed with a roomful of students, celebrating the confirmation in their faith, and the accompanying proud parents. In my hike through Denmark, the Kro hotels have joined McDonald's as dependable hosts.

Kro hotels were given royal privilege by King Erik Klipping in 1286. The story goes that the king was frustrated with a shortage of good accommodation as he travelled throughout Denmark, so he ordered the establishment of a network of these hotels. Now 700 years later, over 100 of the inns remain, and they provide quality food and rooms. I have assumed that the Kro room rates went beyond my budget limits and have not stayed overnight. However, I have enjoyed their coffee or tea and the odd meal in a relaxed break from my constant hiking. Thank you, King Erik Klipping.

Along a major road, in Saggelund I discover a cafeteria that is clean, bright and friendly. I take a tray from the stack and make my way along a counter of food on display. To my delight, they have soup, and I am treated to a big bowl of white asparagus soup with little meatballs – a dish identical to one I enjoyed in the Netherlands a few years back.

A young couple at a nearby table are headed home after a holiday in Hamburg, Germany. They are curious about my backpack sitting on the chair across from me: "That looks heavy. Where are you going with it?" We have a chat about my hike while other diners are craning their necks to hear. I leave the couple with Canada pins and a bookmark showing my book covers. Then I must be a source of chatter as I pass the series of big windows on my way to the road headed south toward Germany.

At the end of a 33-kilometre day, I enter Haderslev as the rain begins, and I locate my hostel for the night. This aged building is the opposite of last night's paradise, and it comes with the smell of stale tobacco smoke at reception. The owners live beyond the office area, and a few teens and children appear at a doorway and then disappear as a man arrives to look after my registration. I seem to be the only guest.

I'm assigned a room so narrow I can't remove my backpack between the wall and two bunk beds but need to back into the hallway to do so. I'm pleased at not having to share this cell as I spread out my things on the extra bed. After my usual shower, I go for a walk through a gentle rain to buy breakfast items at a nearby grocery store.

At this easygoing hostel, the people are friendly, and I have a good sleep. However, I remain perplexed at the differences among this country's Danhostels. Most are clean, bright and airy; this one is not. In its shortcomings, this facility is unique.

Sunday, May 14, 2017

As no breakfast is provided at the hostel, I hit the road by seven in the morning, instead of the nine o'clock start that comes with waiting for an 8:00 am breakfast. The extra two hours put me 10 kilometres down the trail, and the early morning hours always prove to be the less strenuous part of the day's hike. The earlier I start, the easier it seems.

As I travel south, farm crops are further along in their spring growth. The sweet smell of a field of canola wafts toward me, and I notice it is well into the blossom stage.

This is another quiet Sunday where I think of all the families in all those houses as I trudge along. I stop at a church within a cemetery in the community of Hoptrup where a couple and their little daughter are preparing the music and sacred vessels for the service. As in so many Danish churches, the wooden model of a ship is hanging from the middle of the ceiling just above the assembly. The ship models displayed in churches represent women's prayers for the safe return of seafaring men and may have been donated by men in thanks for arriving home after an arduous journey.

During most of my European hikes, businesses have been closed on Sundays. Now I pass an Aldi grocery store that is open, and it even has a bakery area where I can get a fresh cup of coffee. I perch on a roadside curb and finish the items I had started for breakfast early this morning.

In mid-afternoon at the edge of a park with campground, I notice the *Genner Hoel Pandekagehus*, a pancake house where I enjoy the simplest recipe – a pancake as big as my dinner plate and sprinkled with sugar. That, and a fresh cup of coffee, is the perfect meal. The family at the next table mention, "We saw you hike along the road," and now the grandfather and a middle-school-aged granddaughter engage in a conversation with me while the grandmother and younger boy listen. Apparently, when they passed me on the road, the granddaughter asked how far they all thought I would be going. Now they are surprised at my story and the distances I'm covering.

43

I find the use of English in this Danish-speaking country interesting. Many people speak English, often with a quaint accent acquired from a British teacher, and our conversations can be quite straightforward. I continue to take comfort in the fact that I couldn't possibly have learned the dozen languages I have traversed on my thousands of kilometres across Europe. My basic needs can be met through gestures of looking for food (by imitating someone eating), water (by pretending to drink) or a bed for the night (by placing the side of my face against my folded hands). However, it is refreshing to be able to go beyond those actions and to engage in a discussion with a local resident.

I enter the city of Aabenraa and, as usual, follow the GPS instructions on my phone. These lead me to a hidden alley behind a towering church near downtown but with not a hint of a hostel. A young man is getting into his car, and I ask him: "Can you find the local Danhostel on your smart phone? My information doesn't make any sense. It says the hostel should be right here, but none of these buildings look like a hostel."

He is able to find the location on his phone though we don't understand the reason for the electronic confusion. It seems I have another two kilometres to go, for a total of 30 kilometres, and he asks: "Do you want a ride to the hostel?" Of course, as part of my "rules" of hiking every step, I politely refuse and leave him a Canada lapel pin.

The hostel is no longer a Danhostel – a member of the Hostelling International chain. It has become a "campground hotel," and that may have been the reason for the GPS uncertainty. This campground hotel is clean, friendly and efficient, and I don't even have to make my own bed as that has already been done by the housekeeping staff.

As it is located on a fjord, the town features two marinas with dozens of boats in each. I pass these on my way to supper at the "Beach Pit" takeout stand. Their cheeseburger – with its secret special sauce – may be one of the tastiest I've ever had.

I send Joanne a text message: "Over the German border tomorrow will be about 35 km, I think. I'm now at the hostel in Aabenraa."

She replies: "Good one! Mother's Day here. It's going to be a quiet day!" With an ocean between us, I feel so far from home during special events. I think of my seminary days and of missing family activities while I was away for the school year. Now my absence comes with the same longing but with an added twinge of guilt. I should be home, but my strange dream doesn't allow for that.

Then I send Jesper, from back in Aalborg, an email message about leaving his country of Denmark tomorrow. He replies: "Great to hear from you. I hope you enjoyed your 'short time in Denmark.' I read the article [in the Horsens Folkeblad]. Great story. Enjoy your trip south from Denmark. All the best and good luck."

Monday, May 15, 2017

I have my own breakfast so I can start early on today's hike of 38 kilometres. A plastic grocery bag holds my leftover items of cheese and crackers, fruit and a yogurt drink. The "Laughing Cow" cheese is convenient but disappointing – convenient, as the round flat box of wedges in foil take little room; disappointing, because it is the processed variety, far from the Gouda cheese of my youth.

In the countryside I stop for a cup of coffee at a KRO hotel. These hotels have been relaxed and friendly. Now, again, I realize that not everything is perfect everywhere as a strict young woman says: "You only have 10 minutes to drink your coffee because we're busy." The tiny cup of coffee she brings me tastes as old as this well-worn building, and it costs the usual high price that I've experienced throughout Denmark. Food and service is expensive in this country, but this cup of coffee is ridiculous.

The morning opens up to hazy steam clouds serving as foreground to big woollen ones higher up in the mid-blue sky. I pass a wild area of marsh and trees where birds unite in a chirping chorus. Then I stop to take a short video of this sound and see it as a moving farewell to Denmark.

About a year ago, I joined the Conservative Party of Canada in order to stop one of its candidates from winning the leadership race. Before my departure I sent the party contact people an email message asking how to vote from the far reaches of Denmark. They never did reply, and now I realize the vote took place two days ago, and life in Canada goes on.

This area must be riddled with hog farms as the smell of pig manure is constant. I pass fallow fields and wonder when they will be seeded for the next crop. Then a series of anthills at the roadside remind me that I can't see all the communities around me: hidden ones are industrious just below the earth's surface.

As I approach the German border, I stop at the "Grill House" for a coffee and an ice cream cone to celebrate my entering another country. The woman at this take-out stand advises me, "It's 800 metres to the border," and I'm surprised, once again, at the ease with which Europeans cite distances. A

Canadian would be inclined to say, "Oh, about a kilometre" – or, in a built-up area, "A couple of blocks" – but such lack of preciseness would never do in Europe.

I send Joanne a text message: "Less than a km to Germany!" Near the border a "China Transport" truck is parked, and it is striking as the cab is painted in gaudy colours that look like a compilation of cartoon characters.

This is the tenth border I'm crossing on my European hikes, and I think back on those experiences. In all cases, from Portugal to Estonia, the borders were unguarded, and I simply kept hiking. Rarely did the boundary provide a sign of welcome to the next country as the European Union downplayed differences among its member countries. The only indication that I had just left a nation might come from the buzzing of my phone in my pocket when it suggested I purchase access to the next country's network. Now, crossing into Germany, I see a Danish and a German police officer standing on the median as they observe passing cars. They wave me on, and I step onto German soil.

3. Northern Germany

Monday, May 15, 2017 (continued)

On crossing into my next country, I send Joanne a text message: "Just entered Germany!"

Joanne: "Yay!"

Over the border the scenery does not change, but two other things do. Firstly, my iPhone's Danish data and minutes are not usable in Germany, so I cannot count on it to help me find the next hostel. Secondly, the friendly "D-r-r-ring" of a bicycle bell warns me of someone approaching from behind, and a greeting and wave remind me I'm back in this land of courteous cyclists.

Just past the border, a nature trail takes me the last few kilometres into the town of Flensburg. This path consists of a treed slope on my right (with the odd rotten stump for interest) and on my left the Flensburg Firth, an inlet of the Baltic Sea.

The walkway takes me onto a waterside of stone with benches, food vendors and people out for a stroll in the afternoon sunshine. Bicycles make their way through the crowd, and I come closer than ever to being in an accident on my European tour. As two bikes approach from ahead of me, I step aside to let them pass and almost get hit by another two coming up from behind. My fright reteaches a lesson: when walking among Europe's cyclists, don't make any sudden moves. They know what they're doing (I hope!).

I continue along this crescent of concrete around the firth, passing groups lost in conversation on my right while I appreciate the hundreds of sailboats and outboard motorboats at peace on my left. Without access to the Internet, I need to ask several passersby: "Is this the way to the Danhostel?" They express uncertainty, but I seem to have a few kilometres to go.

The seafront ends, and I look for a shortcut to the hostel. This takes me along side streets past factories till I get into a business district and, finally, I locate the hostel in an out-of-the-way lane. The three-storey red-brick structure is located in a park and is advertised to be in a "green relaxing environment." It is welcoming after a 38-kilometre day as are the three guests with whom I share our six-bed room.

For all the technology back in Denmark, I am challenged here: the hostel has no Wi-Fi and a local restaurant only takes cash. I buy a German SIM card at the post office in the Sky grocery store where a clerk needs to phone someone somewhere to activate it, and it won't be functioning till 24 hours have elapsed. (In other countries, this procedure has consisted of entering a code, which activated the SIM card immediately.)

I ask about Internet service in this area, and someone suggests: "You could use the WiFi at Burger King, but it's a few kilometres away." Instead, I try my iPhone outside the grocery store and, luckily, catch a Wi-Fi network to send Joanne a text message: "I'll contact you tomorrow. Will have my data then. No Internet at hostel or restaurants in the area. All is well."

50

In Denmark I saw signs of *"Fodklinik"* (foot clinic), and Joanne has suggested I find someone to treat my feet. The corn on my left little toe and a few blisters make walking a challenge. At the hostel I enquire as to where I might find such a service and also get directions to the city library so I can send my next trek message to family and friends. Then the man at reception suggests Henkelstein restaurant for supper, and I go there for a bowl of soup, a salad and a local Flensburg Beer. To my surprise, this up-to-date eatery takes cash only: credit cards are not accepted.

Tuesday, May 16, 2017

I'm up at 7:00 am to start my wash in the hostel laundry, and breakfast will be available at 7:30. I stand in the building doorway to watch the rain in the trees and appreciate not having to walk through it as I'm taking a rest day.

After using the dryer and folding my clothes, I set out to find the foot clinic in a woman's home in a subdivision. Still without access to data, I have trouble locating this house on the hostel's city map and ask a passerby for directions. This woman is out for a stroll in the rain as she is a part-time teacher and today is her day off. She says: "You have about two kilometres to go. I'll come with you as part of my walk today." A chat about her work, our families and my trek fill the time to my destination.

Arriving at the house, I ring the doorbell, and a woman gets up from working on a client's feet. She says her work day is almost over: "This person is my last appointment for today, but there's another clinic a few blocks away." Following her instructions, I turn left and right for a few blocks.

As I arrive at the house, I notice the first woman pulling up in her car. She has kindly been concerned about my searching in a strange city in the rain. As it turns out, the second woman is busy with a client and booked for the day. She says, "I can give you an appointment for tomorrow," but that won't work for me as I need to continue hiking then.

To avoid another walk in the rain, I catch a bus back to the city centre. There I stop at a McDonald's outlet to have a coffee, enjoy a chocolate McFlurry and use their Wi-Fi for my iPhone. Then I walk to the public library, which is located above a shopping mall, so I can send my "Trek Message 3" by email. I'm impressed with this arrangement, where shoppers simply take an escalator upward to library activities.

As I stroll through the mall before going up to the library, I notice a shop called "New Nails," where the young man at the desk assures me that someone can look after my feet in a few minutes. Then a young woman gestures for me to take a seat in a recliner chair where she soaks my feet in a tub and bathes them. Then she uses little scissors to remove dead skin, and she clips my nails. Finally, she massages and applies a eucalyptus-scented ointment. After all that, I'd like to say that my feet now feel like new, but they're the same old ones. Perhaps, though, they're reinvigorated to do another 1000 kilometres or so.

I use the escalator to go up to the library and wait for a vacant spot among the row of computers. As I type my email message, I'm reminded of difficulties with the German keyboard on my first trek through this country. The computer automatically capitalizes all nouns as is the German way; on the keyboard the location of "Y" and "Z" are reversed, and punctuation symbols are in unusual places. The screen ends up full of squiggly red lines appearing under all the English words, which the computer assumes are misspelled German words. After converting the first letters of nouns into lower case, I go back over the message to make corrections while trying to ignore both the red squiggles and the presence of others waiting their turn for the bank of computers. I need all my concentration to include interesting items in my message while not turning it into gibberish on this German keyboard.

Sometimes the walking is the simple part. More complex are the challenges of maintaining communication with home, adapting to a different hostel bed every night and wondering when the next coffee might appear. In Denmark the milk used for coffee was only 1.5% butterfat; now in Germany it's a little creamier, thank goodness.

I find a bowl of chili at a take-out stand in the mall to serve as my supper. My phone, with its new SIM card, will not work, and I walk down the street to a Sky grocery store near the hostel. I stop at the store's electronics area where the clerk advises, "In Germany you need to unlock the SIM card with a special code," which is something I hadn't experienced elsewhere. The trek continues to be a study in technology, and I let Joanne know of my new phone number, which now starts with "49" in Germany, not with "45" as it did in Denmark.

Wednesday, May 17, 2017

Getting out of the town of Flensburg proves to be complicated, but the GPS information on my iPhone makes it doable. Having arrived in the countryside, I stop at a restaurant, which is a dome of wood and glass but with only a half dozen customers. The waitress tells me that on weekends the place is buzzing, with hundreds of customers and every seat taken.

Well into a series of small fields among stretches of woods, I realize I forgot something back in Flensburg. I obtained a Hostelling International (HI) card at the hostel in Skagen, Denmark at the beginning of this trek. At each Danhostel, I showed the hosteller the card to receive a 10% discount on my lodging.

Now in Germany the HI card is a requirement but does not provide a discount. Here, as well, I need to leave the card at the desk at check-in, and it is returned to me at checkout. I assume this is a method for tracking the guests in case there is misbehaviour or damage. I'm not sure of that, but it does feel like a lack of trust – one that seems unwarranted in the hostels' relaxed atmosphere. In my experience, managers at hostels generally find guests to be well behaved, respectful and cooperative.

The older man, who was looking after the reception area in Flensburg when I left early this morning, didn't mention my membership card left at his desk. I wasn't used to asking for it as that hadn't been required in Denmark. Now I have left it behind and wonder whether that will be a problem at the next hostel.

Gusts blow up from behind me – from the north – and I catch a flash of fluorescent orange out of the corner of my eye. I stop and realize it's the cloth "yield" sign that has been jerked from my backpack and blown into the ditch. I retrieve it and attach the Velcro a bit more firmly. Despite the wind from behind me, I'm starting to feel warm, facing the sun as I head south. For the first time on this trek, I'm perspiring.

I'm pleased with the feeling of freedom as I hike past small fields, herds of a few dozen beef cattle and deciduous woods. In comparison, yesterday's rainy "rest day" in Flensburg felt restrictive. Now I'm out here hiking while, back in Canada, our daughter Shanna is home with our little granddaughter. I concentrate on my hike as I realize my longing for home can use valuable energy. I take a break on the top step of a stairway that leads down to the road under an overpass. Then, after a rest and a snack, I keep walking.

At the end of 36 kilometres, I arrive in the town of Schleswig. Without an HI card, I can't stay in the hostel here, and I don't want to pay for a new card. The woman on duty at the hostel arranges to get a scanned copy of my HI card sent to her from the hostel in Flensburg, and she convinces them to send the card to the hostel in the city of Kiel where I'll be staying two nights from now. She comments: "The card is always given back to the client at checkout. I'm surprised the man in Flensburg didn't pass it to you. Maybe he was tired."

I try to hurry in making these arrangements at the hostel reception desk because a line of middle-school-aged children is forming behind me. Each child is eager to ask a question of the woman managing the place for the evening. These requests often have to do with asking for a piece of play equipment kept in the office area, such as ping-pong paddles.

After finally settling into my private room, I go in search of supper. I'm impressed with everything in the neighbourhood. Next to the hostel is a similar red-brick structure from which classical music wafts into the evening. I understand a local orchestra of adults and teens is practicing for an upcoming concert.

A few doors down, I pass a modern pool-sauna facility and decide it is worth a look. The young man at the desk is enthusiastic about the facility: "The construction and operating costs are covered by the 'energy savings' system." I'm not sure what that means, but it seems to have worked as this white, spotless building is impressive.

I walk a few blocks to the Famila grocery store. In the delicatessen I gather items as my supper – pickled herring, olives, potato salad, chicken strips and tomato juice. I pay for these at the checkout counter and take them to the café just inside the store entrance. This posh area is adjacent to the bakery, which includes a takeout service for drinks and ice cream, and it is the homiest such area I've seen. It consists of sleek wooden tables and upholstered chairs among a set of partitions with bookshelves of volumes to read and artwork to enjoy. The area continues outside the store entrance where it becomes a patio with lawn furniture.

Thursday, May 18, 2017

On the way out of the hostel in the morning, the person on duty gives me the photocopy of my HI card that arrived from Flensburg. I can temporarily use this in place of my actual card, which will – hopefully – join me in Kiel.

It is a hot day, and I change into my shorts by mid-morning. From my walking world, I look out at the vehicles, and I'm impressed with two facts: the cars are fast, and the tractors are big. Since starting this trek in Denmark, I hadn't seen cars speed the way they did in Portugal and Poland. Now that's changing, and people seem to be in a hurry to get somewhere. At the same time, tractors working the fields are modern – with the driver looking small in an oversized cab. I grew up on a farm, so I'm familiar with much to do with agriculture. However, many tractors here are giants with mysterious equipment attached at front or back and with tires that tower over my head.

This morning I stopped at an area of stores that included a *"Blumenautomat"* (flower dispensing machine). Now I pass a dairy farm where a roadside sign advertises a *"Milch Tankstelle"* (milk station). At the entrance to the dairy building, a customer can lift the door on a contraption, place a bottle on the tray and deposit a few coins. Then the bottle fills with fresh milk, and the person might also buy eggs, butter or other items from a nearby coin-operated machine. These units are a popular source of dairy products given the number of them I've seen advertised.

Along the route a sign with hiking information includes the blue and yellow stylized shell that I saw so often on Spain's pilgrimage route, the Camino de Santiago de Compostela. I only see this one symbol, so it must have been a local person's dream to make this part of a pilgrimage route.

At the end of a 27-kilometre hike, I reach the town of Eckernförde and get another view of the Baltic Sea. This is a touristy area of beach chairs, pale sand and food stalls. However, the season is just starting, so crowds have not yet arrived. A few people are seeking information at the tourist centre on the beach, and I join them to ask about a bed for the night as there is no hostel in this town. They suggest the inexpensive Eckotel and make a reservation for me.

Outside the tourism office, I meet a talkative young man getting off his bike. He says: "I'm going into the centre to get a squirrel souvenir for my Australian girlfriend." I don't get to ask about this interesting purchase because he's already into the next topic: "A friend of mine writes about his hikes in many parts of Europe. He doesn't do any long distances – just shorter trails." I hand him a bookmark showing my book covers and indicating where these works are available in case he or his friend is interested in following up.

I hike the kilometre or so into town and enter an area of stores and small industry. I am concerned that Eckotel might be second-rate in this setting, but it is a charming little place. A central structure with lots of windows and a few tables will serve as breakfast area in the morning and provides Wi-Fi access for this evening. A couple of wings feature rooms that are simple but clean and homey. I find a nearby Famila grocery store, purchase supper in their deli and eat it in their cozy setting of tables and chairs.

Friday, May 19, 2017

In the morning I look for Andre, the hotel owner, so I can pay my bill. I find him in a corner office of a building next to the hotel where his business partner runs a shop that sells ceramic tiles. Andre sports a ponytail and is proud of his travel experiences: "A few years ago, I rode my vintage motorbike through Canada and the USA." He is an easy conversationalist, and we share stories of life on the road.

Then I head out on my quiet path into the country where, as on previous spring hikes, I see signs for fresh *Spargel* (white asparagus) for sale. I approach a railway track when the familiar ringing of the crossing bells alerts me to a coming train. I grab my iPhone to snap a picture, but – given the speed reached by German trains – I only catch its departure. Since the front and rear of the train look alike, it could be assumed from the photo that I caught the image as the train approached. But, truthfully, I was late and barely caught its rear as it streaked into the distance.

Several times people have mentioned that a town is, for example, 10 "miles" away rather than 16 "kilometres." They assume we use "miles" in Canada, which is understandable since we're still unsettled about the whole metric thing.

This morning I felt a cool breeze as I passed another beach area waiting for tourists, but by noon I changed into my shorts. Meanwhile, the sky has gone from having clouds of mist to fluffy elephants and whales – or maybe I've been alone too long.

The terrain is a mixture of woods and crops with more huge tractors using the roadway to go from field to field. I have yet to see any long-distance hikers, just a biker or two every 10 or 15 minutes.

The 31 kilometres to the city of Kiel prove to be a long hike. Some days seem longer than others, for no known reason. The tiresomeness of a hike has less to do with hills or traffic and more to do with my mindset. If I cannot remain mentally and physically energized, 20 kilometres can feel like 40 of them.

As I approach the city, I am reminded of a message from Joanne that mentioned a young man from Kiel who was an Airbnb visitor at our house last week. Since I did not get the chance to meet this guest, I won't bother trying to find him here, but I continue to marvel at how small a world we inhabit.

When I arrive at the hostel in Kiel, my Hostelling International card is waiting for me. The attendant comments: "I'm glad someone arrived to claim it." The hostel is lacking a social atmosphere, and I hear some grumbling because the Wi-Fi is not free and is not available throughout the building.

Instead, we are limited to using the Wi-Fi in the lobby and at a cost of one Euro for a four-hour period.

My boots have become a problem. They have not maintained their rigidity, and the heels have been wearing more quickly than they normally should. At a 15-minute walk from the hostel, I locate Unterwegs, a store that sells hiking equipment, and there I meet the perfect salesperson.

Johannes is a friendly, but business-like, young man, and I tell him about my trek through Europe. He takes one look at my footwear and says: "You have the wrong boots. See how I can bend the soles. These were made for hiking and climbing in rough areas. You need boots with stiff soles so your feet do not bend with each step of your fast hike." I now realize that the tendons in my feet have been complaining because of the repeated flexing of these boots over long distances.

Then Johannes shows me how to tie my boots. After more than 6,000 kilometres across Europe, I'm sure I have nothing else to learn. However, I am now shown that making a double starting knot halfway up the lacing allows me to split the top and bottom halves of the bootlaces so I can tie those two independently of each other. In this way, I can make the bottom as tight as I want and then tie the top so it is comfortable.

I also buy some hiker's wool to avoid abrasion between my toes, and I get three pairs of socks. Johannes recommends the socks that come as "right" and "left." I have seen these elsewhere and have considered them a novelty item. In fact, these socks are shaped to one's right and left foot and avoid the bunching of extra sock material at the toes. Such things are significant when you hike up to 40 kilometres a day. Then everything has to fit properly.

I have a hankering for spaghetti, and Vapiano's fits the bill. This restaurant is a few blocks from the hostel, and I arrive there after taking a bridge towering over rail lines and a lift bridge over the *Nord-Ostsee-Kanal* ("Kiel Canal," in English). The Kiel Canal is a 98-kilometre-long freshwater seaway that links the North Sea at Brunsbüttel to the Baltic Sea at Kiel. In the near distance on my right a couple of freighters lie tied in the harbour that is part of the canal as it prepares to join the Baltic Sea.

Vapiano's is buzzing with a Friday evening crowd. People make their way to the service counter where half a dozen cooks prepare dishes to customers' specifications and add fresh herbs from potted plants growing at the ready. My spaghetti tastes fine though I lack enthusiasm for the time and inconvenience of standing in line and waiting for the dish to be ready. It's an interesting concept, but not one I appreciate.

At the hostel I place my old boots and socks in the room's garbage pail, take a picture and wish them good riddance. During the night the crackling of a thunderstorm brings me wide awake. I get up to stand at the window and fully enjoy the distant flashes.

Saturday, May 20, 2017

In the morning I feel like a man with new boots. Okay, I am a man with new boots. I notice an immediate improvement in how my feet feel: the boots are snug but comfortable.

In this part of Germany, I see few McDonald's outlets. To my disappointment, Burger King is the diner of choice. These eateries seem to be everywhere and come with tiny electric cars as the delivery fleet.

As I use a crosswalk and pass in front of cars stopped for a red light, I continue to feel uneasy. Many engines shut off as an energy-saving measure, and I feel threatened by the fact that they might suddenly roar to life. This is a needless worry, but it remains disconcerting to walk in front of a row of these potential attackers. In my walking environment, it's another thing that takes some adjustment in my subconscious.

Among a series of shops at the edge of the town of Preetz, my eye catches a bright café that deals in coffee and ice cream – the perfect combination. Eva, the owner, is from Bulgaria and her husband is from this area. Eva speaks English well, and she tells an interesting tale: "When I met my future husband, I didn't speak German, and he didn't speak Bulgarian. We both knew basic English, so that's what we used. And we still do, twenty years later." Eva says her husband has mentioned writing a book about his interesting life, so I chat about the need for people to write their stories. I leave her one of my bookmarks with contact information that he can use to contact me about writing if he would like.

On my way through the town of Preetz, I stop on a bridge to watch several families appear from under this rock structure in canoes. They are lost in conversation as the paddles maintain their rhythm. They slide under overhanging branches into the distance as I recall my own canoeing experiences on various Canadian lakes. They seem so much more relaxed than I in my rigorous journey.

As I set off again, I think of the restrictions of my trek. I'm imprisoned of my own will: I walk and sleep and eat, and I focus on not going outside of those limits. I simply need to keep going.

My mind wanders to a different look at my hike. I recall my lack of athletic interest and ability in my youth, and I wonder if people compensate for childhood shortcomings by overdoing their adult interests. I imagine this process is similar to a swimmer soaring out of the water. If the person goes down to the bottom of the pool and jumps upward, it is possible to leave the bounds of the water. It seems that the lower we start, the higher we can rise. And, with thousands of European hiking kilometres behind me, I continue to rise to unusual heights.

The majority of the trees in the passing woods are deciduous, with conifers choosing the upper ridges. The aromas in rural areas alternate among those produced by sweet canola, sour ensilage, pig manure and chemical sprays. My sense of smell is constantly pulled in different directions.

I have seen several patches of flowers where customers could cut their own bouquets and leave cash for the owner. Now I pass another of these and walk up to it for a closer look. The sign reads, *"Blumen selbst schneiden,"* (cut-your-own flowers) and lists prices for sunflowers, gladioli, lilies and tulips. Under the sign is a concrete box with a slot for *"Kasse"* (cash), and it occurs to me that such trust exists in rural areas everywhere – the belief that people will deposit the correct payment.

I stop at an oriental restaurant for wanton soup, krupuk (deep fried crackers) and jasmine tea. This nourishes me for the last of my 30 kilometres to the town of Plön. I continue to find quiet communities joined by quiet roads till traffic becomes heavier about five kilometres before Plön, a tourism haven built on strips of peninsula and isthmus. The bridges into the community are being renovated, and no walkway is available for pedestrians. My only access to town seems to be via a bridge under construction. It is Saturday, and there are no workers present to stop me, so I use this unfinished structure to find my way into town.

The hostel is serving several sets of teenagers, none of whom looks at a phone as they engage in planned and spontaneous games. Often groups at hostels have made arrangements to be served supper during their stay. That is the case today, and I pay a few euros to join them.

A local orchestra, with a choir of teenagers, practices on the ground floor of the building, so I perch at a picnic table outside this area. I use my iPhone to make a short video of the hostel lawn and shrubbery with this delightful music and singing in the background.

In the evening a group of the young people sit in a circle on the lawn and sing rounds of a traditional German song while they record their performance on a smart phone. It gets darker, and a vigorous game of hide-and-seek breaks out. Then the well-behaved group of teenagers of this afternoon turns into a raucous throng into the night.

Sunday, May 21, 2017

The teenaged guests kept at their hide-and-seek game – with accompanying shouts and stampedes – till 3:00 am. Now the sleepy bunch can relax on this quiet Sunday while I have to keep walking. I have already forgiven them for keeping me awake through the night, and I wish I could stay. They are a relaxed mix of young men and women – so refreshing in comparison to my introverted personality within a male group of earnest seminarians during my teens.

I assume there is a biker rally somewhere: over the course of the day, close to 1000 motorbikes vroom past. However, a local person says this activity is a Sunday routine as so many people own souped-up motorcycles in this part of Germany.

As I hike through a wooded area, a man gets off his bicycle to study his map. He says he's from the province of Groningen in the Netherlands and switches to the Dutch language when I tell him I speak it as well. He asks which road to take to some distant town, but I can't help him since I hardly know where I am myself. He mentions that – at 70 years of age – he's pleased to be healthy enough to pedal a circuit of the area, and I tell him: *"Zo oud ben ik ook"* (I'm that age as well).

His next words are lost in the whine of two motor scooters racing to pass a car. He has some unkind Dutch words for them as more motorbikes fly by, making us feel vulnerable on this narrow road. It would have been nice to have a Dutch conversation with him, but the background noise doesn't allow for it, so we go on our way.

In the community of Klein, I'm reminded of the various ways people here try to stay physically fit. A sign advertising a business called *"Zentrum für Kung Fu & Bewegungskünste"* (centre for kung fu and exercise arts) shows an extensive list of offerings: kung fu, kickboxing, children's kung fu, tai chi, yoga, children's yoga, pilates, occupational therapy and sauna. For now, I'll stick with my own workout of day-long hikes.

I pass a business called "American Diner" and go in to take a look. The place is decorated in red and white with lots of chrome and, even, a jukebox from the 1950's. I order a chocolate milkshake and sit among the groups of customers with their glasses of beer. This is an odd setting in rural Germany, and I half expect a film director to yell, "Cut!"

An hour or so later, I stop at a hotel restaurant for a coffee break. The owner sports a stained apron in his cluttered kitchen. He is enthused about this unusual customer and doesn't want to be paid for the very tasty cup of coffee.

A parade of a dozen antique tractors, with families clambered aboard, remind me I've returned to farm country. Nearby hay is being fluffed up in preparation for baling, and another large field of barley appears. Away from town my Internet reception is inconsistent.

Then I meet a young man named Cai who is out for a bike ride: "I'm taking a break from my wife and kids." He mentions a path around a nearby lake – his favourite trail in the area. He is as unsuccessful in convincing me to take this detour as others have been throughout Europe.

At the end of a 34-kilometre day, I arrive in the town of Bad Segeberg. The hostel is located near the downtown area but across the street from a campground. It seems to be deserted, which is unusual for a hostel: when I ring the doorbell, it isn't answered. Two elderly couples are immersed in a lawn bowling game on the green next door, and I ask: "Do you know anything about the hostel? Is it closed?" One of the women seems familiar with the place and accompanies me back to it. She rings the bell, and this time a man comes to the door, so she returns to her lawn bowling.

The man, who seems to be the owner, has been working inside the building to get ready for a crowd of young people arriving tomorrow. At times hostellers have suggested that I reserve a bed in advance, and he joins that group by reminding me that I shouldn't be *"spontan"* (spontaneous). My tired look must have led him to give me a room, but he says that no breakfast will be provided, which is understandable.

I celebrate the opening of a second bottle of Camp Suds for my shower. Such an occasion – which would be routine at home – marks another milestone in my trek. Since I brought three bottles, I must be a third of the way through this hike. This serves as a tangible sign of my progress, which often seems illusory.

As I leave the hostel to find some supper, I take a closer look at its outdoor area. Tables in need of paint and repair are spread across the back lawn, and the flags in front of the building are tattered. Throughout Europe I have been surprised at the differences among hostels. Most are wonderful; a few are in desperate need of attention.

This day is complete when I find a bowl of *Spargelsuppe* (asparagus soup) and a plate of spaghetti at a bar a few blocks away. Then I return to be alone in this big building, and I have an excellent sleep.

Monday, May 22, 2017

I awake at 4:30 and, with no breakfast served at the hostel, hit the trail by 5:30. I relish these early morning hours and stop to take a picture of the sunrise. By quarter to six, the clerk in a bakeshop is handing me a marzipan *Copenhagener* (Danish pastry) and a cup of coffee. At such an early hour, the street is already busy with workers making their way to the stores and stopping for a coffee at the bakery. I pass a house with walls of red bricks, sandwiched between boards at various angles, and with a plaque showing it was built in 1541. In Canadian terms, that's an incredibly long time ago, being seven years after Jacques Cartier reached "New France."

With the early morning hours – before my mind becomes cluttered with detail – comes a philosophical bent in me. My brain produces a series of disorganized thoughts: I realize the trek also takes place inside of me; I notice that it's my hands on the hiking poles that set the pace more than my legs do. I ponder that I'm not a hero as some seem to imply; rather, we are all heroes on some level. Then my mind responds to the vegetation in roadside ditches with a touch of humour: "When all else is gone, there'll still be dandelions."

I head into the country where the bicycle path follows a ridge overlooking the road so I gaze down at car roofs as they pass. Here massive fields include potatoes, corn, barley, asparagus and strawberries. At many farms the sour smell of ensilage wafts toward me while the blades of another row of wind turbines turn lazily in the distance.

I've been struggling to find an answer to the question I've been asked so often: "On your hikes do you get lonely?" This time I've concentrated on that question, and I've concluded I'm definitely alone but do not feel lonely. I miss much from my life back home – Joanne, our home and its conveniences; not having to look for a bed each day; not having to adapt to another culture, another language and another type of food. In light of all these, the walking is the lesser challenge, and it's the living that's difficult. I take comfort in the fact that my booklet of notes is now half full, which shows I am moving along through this trek.

By 9:45 am, I've already done 16 kilometres when I arrive in a built-up area that I assume to be the community of Nahe. I look for something to eat and stop at a bakery where I'm told: "No, this isn't Nahe; that's the next place. We have pizza here if you want some for lunch." I order a slice, but it's served cold as they have no microwave oven. Cold pizza is not food; it is desperation.

At the edge of the community of Alsterwiesen, I come upon an older structure that provides an outdoor café on its lawn. This square two-storey wooden building seems to house a couple of workshops. After a cup of coffee, I take a peek in one of the large doorways and find a young woman making furniture from pieces out of a pile of used wooden items. She points to a table she has just finished, and it looks quaint and interesting with hints of the wood's previous role as a door poking through.

I've noticed the repeated use of car horns in this area. Their use seems to reflect local custom: for days I hear no car horns; then I hear several honks, one after the other. They are either desperate pleas for people to get out of the way or expressions of frustration in heavy traffic.

Each gas station in this part of Germany has an area with drinks and snacks – like a mini-McDonald's. These places are clean and comfortable with a few tables and stools, a coffee machine and a fridge of cold drinks. I stop at one of these cafés, and Kajsa, the young woman at the counter, advises me on hotels in the area. In her practised English, she adds: "I really enjoyed a trip through the Orient a few years ago. I learned so much about the way other people live." We have a chat about travelling, and Kajsa seems pleased with this diversion from the monotony of taking people's payment for their gasoline fill-ups.

I thought I might complete the 56 kilometres to the hostel in Hamburg today. However, as I enter the city of Norderstedt 35 kilometres into the day, a small hotel seems the ideal place to stop for the night. Zur Glashütte Hotel is a family-run business where the son shows me my room. Daniel, his sister and their father are great hosts, providing a spotless home away from home, as well as relaxed conversation about my hike and about this part of Germany. For such a small hotel, it is busy, and I am assigned their last bed. Apparently, most of the guests are construction workers who need to get to work early, so breakfast will start at 6:00 am, much to my delight.

The hotel also sports a small restaurant, and I have a turkey salad as my supper. I head back to my room and have a drink – one that I didn't know was a drink when I bought it earlier today. You see, at a grocery store checkout, a display of liqueur-filled chocolates grabbed my attention as a good treat for later in the day. Now, after my hotel supper, I open the box of four long tasty chocolates and find out that they are not chocolates at all but tiny bottles of liqueur. I'm disappointed, but drink two of them – just for spite.

Tuesday, May 23, 2017

At the hotel desk, Daniel's sister Steffi is enthralled with the story of my trek, and I leave her three Canada lapel pins and a bookmark. When I leave the hotel, it is garbage collection day and I stop to marvel at the complex mechanism of a truck that picks up the householders' curbside trash containers and empties them into a vehicle's hopper without human help.

I hike through Norderstedt and, 20 minutes later, into the city of Hamburg. I thought I would be seeing some countryside before getting into Hamburg. However, from the hotel onward it was continuous urban landscape, through which I struggle for 21 kilometres of sidewalks, cars and stoplights to arrive at Auf dem Stintfang Hostel where I had stayed on my first trek going eastward through Hamburg.

Arriving at the four-storey sand-coloured brick complex, I climb the series of steps to the hostel entrance and stop outside the glass doors for some private reflection. Here I am, standing at the spot where I arrived on May 1st, five years ago, during my 6,000-kilometre hike from Portugal to Estonia. I am delighted to reach this crossing of the "X" in my two treks across Europe.

The groups of teenagers passing on their way out for a smoke or a walk must wonder about the old man standing here with tears in his eyes. I have a momentary thought for the people who have helped me get to this point, and I still can't understand what this is all about. Then, sporting backpack and hiking poles, as well as a smile of accomplishment, I enter the building to ask for a bed.

In our six-bed room, the three lower beds are taken by Stephen, Judith and an elderly man, so I'm relegated to a top bunk. Age and top bunks don't go together well. I no longer have a young person's flexibility in climbing up and down that ladder. And, at my age, there's a lot of climbing up and down to go pee.

I decide to stay here for two nights, so I order two breakfasts and two suppers at the hostel desk. The first supper is a delicious meal of spaghetti – one of my favourites. Other guests must also have a fondness for this dish, as the dining area is hopping.

After supper I start my laundry in one of the hostel's several machines and stroll down to the Alter Elbe Tunnel. I admire the arched stone entrance to the passageway, in which an elevator for people goes downward through a scary silo-like structure. Apparently, the elevators for vehicles are being renovated, so they are closed, and only pedestrians can take this shortcut under the Elbe River. I recall my previous arrival out of the dark, sombre tunnel into a square drenched in sunshine and featuring loudspeakers and crowds that were the May Day workers' celebration of May 1, 2012. I gaze at the scene into which I emerged five years ago: now I see only the odd tourist and some parked cars – but, certainly, no crowds. Then I take a few photos so I can compare the two experiences later when I'm home and reliving this trek.

In celebration of reaching this crossing point, I go for a drink at the hostel bar, and a sign on the counter advertises the "Sportsman" cocktail. The young man, who serves as bartender, tells me: "I think you'd like the Sportsman. It's a mix of alcohol and citrus juices." Presumably, this alcoholic drink has the redeeming quality of providing a bit of Vitamin C. In any case, it tastes great.

I'm surprised that I encounter no Canadians here; perhaps, they'll arrive in a month or two when summer gets underway. Now, all guests seem to be people from here in Germany. On the way back up to my room, I take the elevator, which I'm sure I deserve.

Wednesday, May 24, 2017

After the extensive hostel breakfast of cereal, meat, cheese, fruit and yogurt within a bustling swarm of young people, I go shopping. Locating a SportScheck store, I purchase two black rubber tips for my hiking poles. Mine are badly worn, and the man who helps me find new ones mentions: "You have Sport Chek stores in Canada, but that's a different company." In its hiking section, this store features an

72

arched bridge that holds a variety of surfaces: rough stones, thin logs and smooth rocks. Walking across these with the boots you are looking to buy will ensure they are appropriate for the terrain you will be crossing.

Throughout Europe I have encountered thousands of dogs. If not on a leash or behind a gate, these animals have tested my fear, which may well come from a youth of dogs nipping and yelping at my heels as I biked home from school. Now in Hamburg I notice that each dog being taken for a walk stays beside its human but with no leash connecting the two. The dogs must be trained to stay close because I never see one stray.

I make my way to the Hamburg Central Library to type "Trek Message 4" to family and friends back home. On my way to the Internet area, I am enthralled by a series of conveyor belts holding a smattering of books and running at odd angles up into the next floor of the building. Clients return their reading material into a chute, and the automated system takes the books into that part of the building where they are housed. I am told that the apparatus comes from Denmark, and I'm not surprised given the degree of innovation I saw as I hiked through that country.

As a non-resident, I'm consigned to using the coin-operated computer station rather than joining the locals at the row of terminals that are free of charge. The email trek message I send Joanne for distribution serves as tentative contact with family and friends. However, it also serves to remind me that home is so far away. This time I realize that Joanne will soon be going to see our son Trevor while he is in Toronto for meetings. And tomorrow I'll keep hiking.

Thursday, May 25, 2017

After breakfast I leave the hostel to get back on my path as I follow the GPS route on my iPhone. It leads me past the wire mesh fence on an overpass to which are attached a series of "love locks" – padlocks that sweethearts fasten to symbolize their love. As I near the crossing of the Elbe River, I realize I'm not headed toward a bridge but, rather, a ferry terminal. With my resolve to walk every step of the way, I need to avoid this ferryboat and to look for a bridge to cross.

The nearest bridge is five kilometres to the east, and I head in that direction. Today is Ascension Thursday, a German holiday, so the streets are deserted as I head through a business section along the Elbe River. This brings me to a set of three bridges for cars, trains and pedestrians respectively. Just across the river, three men are immersed in fashioning curbs for a new road, so I wish them, *"Guten Tag,"* (good day). I notice a nearby hotel café and stop for coffee served in a glass: somehow, the transparency of the glass makes it taste even better.

In Germany this Feast of the Ascension of Jesus into Heaven (40 days after Easter) is celebrated as *Vatertag* (Father's Day). Stories about the origin of this celebration vary: it may have had to do with gifts being given to fathers after the Ascension Day street parades back in the 18th century. Another legend tells of fathers slaughtering animals in spring, taking hams or roasts to the priest and, together, celebrating a break from their work. No matter the origin of this holiday, it includes both large and small groups of men biking together, as well as the occasional woman or family.

On the way to the town of Harburg, I pass through the south end of Hamburg, and this area – with its weeds and worn buildings – seems much poorer than did the central city. I planned to make the hostel in the city of Geesthacht my next stop but the receptionist at the hostel in Hamburg told me it was no longer available as a hostel. Instead, it is now used to house refugee families, and I'm pleased to hear that such a welcoming home is available to a people that have lived in unrest. I'm happy to give up a spot there for someone in greater need and to redirect my path toward the city of Winsen, which will have a small hotel to accommodate me.

A pleasant walk takes me along a bike path for 17 kilometres of hiking on the leeward western side of the grassy dike along the Elbe River. Occasionally I climb the dike to peer over its side and discover a few moored motorboats, people fishing with rod and reel or the odd community huddled on the opposite river bank.

On the trail a few men are resting on a park bench with their bikes parked nearby. One of them asks: "Where are you from?" Then he shouts at friends biking on a parallel path across a field: "Canada!" It's as though they're claiming me as their prize.

I stop at a café, take my place within the chattering crowd and send Joanne a text message: "It's Father's Day in Germany, so I just had a big piece of chocolate cake (and coffee, of course) at a roadside café." It only seems fitting to join the local people in celebration.

In order to have sustenance available throughout this day of mobile celebrations, people follow the tradition of pulling *Bollerwagen* (handcarts) loaded with food and drink. I come upon two of these – one pulled by a family, the other by a group of young women.

In Winsen I arrive at a hotel with a bas-relief of a horse on its front lawn. It seems like a nice place but has no vacancy. The staff direct me a few blocks further to the Hotel am Schlossplatz, or "Hotel Schloss" as the locals call it. As I approach this home for the night, a community celebration takes up the width of the street with food stands, rides and carnival barkers. The front of the hotel is hidden from my view by one of the displays. When I realize I must have passed that goal, I ask a couple who give me vague instructions: "It's back that way on the right." Eventually, I find the hotel among the partygoers and the racket. I'm exhausted after a full day of hiking 37 kilometres and welcome a comfortable, reasonably quiet, room at the back of the building.

After I settle into my quarters and take a shower, the Dutch part of me is drawn to the stand across from the hotel. This kiosk is topped with a model windmill, and I order a feed of ten *Poffertjes*. These simple, tiny pancakes – common in the Netherlands and further afield – are drizzled with melted butter and icing sugar, and they are yummy.

Then I go for a walk to see how I might fit into the excitement of the evening. The main feature of this celebration is noise: everyone talks at once, piped-in music is at full volume and the carnival rides produce shouts and screams. I use the microphone on my iPhone to send Joanne some sample soundscapes, and I ask her: "Do you think I'll be able to sleep tonight? The hotel is in the middle of the activity!"

Three young men must have had an extra drink or two. They have their arms around each other's shoulders so they can stay upright as they make their way through the crowd. One of them trips and starts to collapse, but the others hold him up while a man, who pushes a stroller holding a toddler, frowns at them. I return to the sobriety of my hotel room where, thankfully, the distant noise abates at 10:00 pm, and I get a good night's sleep.

Friday, May 26, 2017

Before breakfast is served at the hotel, I go outside to see the results of last night's revelry. Using WhatsApp, I send Joanne another sample of the sound that has now become a quiet area of workers cleaning up empty bottles and debris stretched across a forlorn park: "That's what it sounded like at 7:00 am."

On my first trek across this part of Europe, each eatery had a combination of a radio blaring American hits and a television set showing a news report or soap opera. So far on this hike, I see little of that, much to my relief. I don't know why restaurants are now quieter – as is the one at "Hotel Schloss" – but I'm grateful as that makes it easier to concentrate on the meal and one's thoughts.

However, the use of car horns has not diminished and feels like a show of superiority by drivers when they are not pleased with the actions of bikers or with my slowness in crossing a road. If cars knew how far I was hiking, they would likely give me leeway. I might then graduate from nuisance to hero.

I just don't seem to be behaving in the way drivers would like. They show their dominance in the species, and I decide hikers should be equipped with horns that are just as loud. That might level the hierarchy of cars coming first, then motorbikes, trucks, bicycles and pedestrians – in that order. I'm still not comfortable with the German language; but, at least, I should be able to show my displeasure with the cars flying by. Perhaps I could pick up one or two German swear words.

I've started to see crops of wheat and endless rows of something I thought was cabbage. I go down into a roadside field and realize those are not young cabbage plants but sugar beets. I'm impressed with the way our memories are stored: my recognition of sugar beet seedlings comes from our fields of those plants back in 1955, when I was eight years old. Here crops seem of a poorer quality than were those further north, with a collection of weeds in a juvenile field of corn.

I pass a sign for the upcoming Roncalli Circus in Hamburg. I have seen similar signs for a different company, Nordens Største Cirkus, back in Denmark. That must be a common form of entertainment in this part of Europe as such signs are widespread on this trek.

With the new tips on my hiking poles and with constant access to data, this is proving to be a good day. Then I approach a large brick building in the community of Radbruck. A roadside sign promises a cup of tea in its café. However, it looks dark and spooky, and a dog guards the entrance, so I speed out of there – with no cup of tea.

Today was warm enough to start the morning in shorts. Now the clouds dissipate, and the GPS directs me onto a single paved lane with gravel shoulders. This must be a shortcut between two towns as the road is busy with cars having to pull onto the shoulder to pass each other. That is a challenge, especially when the cars are passing me at the same time. A couple stops to ask for directions to a plant nursery, and I tell them: "In Canada I could help you, but not here.'"

The soil seems dry, and I see my first irrigation plume in the distance as another huge, scary tractor whizzes past. The sky is clear, with only a few wisps on the horizon. Out in the country, my Internet reception becomes slow, and I need to wait a few moments while the phone decides which road I should take.

In the community of Vögelsen I stop at a backyard café to enjoy chocolate-almond cake and a big cup of coffee under 180-year-old oak trees while my bare feet rest on the chair opposite. Iris is the owner of this hideaway, "Lodencafé Dorfstrasse 9," and I'm the only customer. Iris explains: "This is my retirement project and a way for other people to enjoy this peaceful setting. I like to see travellers stop here to relax, and sometimes I'm vey busy, with all the tables being used." Her neat clothes, careful English and charming dishes suggested she is a refined person. I'm relieved that she doesn't hover but leaves me alone to unwind in this idyllic setting.

As I enter the town of Lüneburg, I pass a community of old vans and gadgets that has the appearance of a hippie commune. In a residential area, I pass a cigarette dispensing machine that precludes the need to travel to a distant store for one's supply. Then I get to the hostel, which looks attractive but has no vacancy. The manager suggests Hotel Zur Hasenburg, a kilometre down the road.

So, this 24-kilometre day ends at a little hotel in Lüneburg as there was no room for me in the hostel. The hotel owner is relaxed despite an "after wedding party" of a few hundred people who are enjoying kebabs prepared by a caterer at a smoking barbecue. I ask the owner which young couple is the bride and groom, and he answers: "It's those older people, and it's not their first time."

After supper at an outside picnic table under an umbrella, I join the half dozen locals gathered at the bar for a drink of *Korn* liquor. The discussion leads to questions about the route I'm following, and twice I go up to my room to retrieve another map that will help resolve the controversy.

At least half the wedding guests spend the evening outside smoking cigarettes while smart phones throughout the gathering are taking pictures. Though the music becomes more subdued at 1:00 am, crowd noises continue till about 2:30. I thoroughly enjoy the experience, despite the lack of sleep.

Saturday, May 27, 2017

In the morning, the owner again expresses his appreciation of my hiking efforts and refuses to charge me for last evening's two beers, two *Korn* drinks and plate of spaghetti with spinach. He reminds me so much of the relaxed hotel owner at the Hotel Stemmann in Buxtehude on my first trek going from west to east through this area. In fact, the town of Buxtehude is only 50 kilometres northeast of this spot.

Normally, I pay close attention to the GPS on my iPhone as it might show another point at which I need to turn. Now, once I'm outside Lüneburg, the information on my device shows that I am to hike straight ahead toward the town of Uelzen, with no turns, for 26 kilometres – the record to date.

I come across another example of the German tradition of planting trees close to the road. One of these holds a cross indicating a death along this narrow stretch – one of all too many I've seen throughout Europe. A few kilometres along, I come across a van of the *Polizei* (police), and two men are setting up a tripod on which is perched an electronic unit to catch speeders. I wave, but they are too busy with this apparatus to care about a Canadian hiker crawling along. To them the cars racing by are much more interesting.

I stop at an outside eatery for a coffee when an elderly man arrives by bike. He's doing a tour of the region and says he has biked long distances for many years. Now, at 85 years of age, he is using a bicycle with a power-assist device. His tone of voice is apologetic, but I tell him: "At your age, that makes sense."

A few kilometres further along, someone at a stand is selling an item we Dutch folks savour and call *"gerookte paling"* (smoked eel). Having purchased this oily product in its plastic wrapping, I realize it would be awkward and messy to eat it while walking. I see a park area located half a block down a side street. There are no picnic tables, but I find a flat sawed-off tree trunk, and there I party. A stream runs by, meters away, and I make my way down to wash my hands of the lingering smell. These few moments become a highlight of this trek.

This morning started cloudy, but by afternoon the sun is beating down. A 32-kilometre hike brings me to Uelzen and a homey hostel with a group of mid-teen girl guides organizing their activities. The manager/receptionist/cook serves a delicious *spaetzle*. I've never cared for these homemade noodles, but these are smothered in perfectly flavoured pieces of chicken in a white sauce, and they are delicious.

Sunday, May 28, 2017

I'm sad to be leaving as this hostel has provided me with a relaxed setting while groups of teenage girls and a few families milled about. The staff had quiet voices that added to the peaceful atmosphere.

This community must be a hub for trains as I heard many go by the hostel through the night and now they pass as I hike. It should be a good morning with a cool wind from the east and some hazy clouds.

At this point my hiking has become automatic: I walk briskly without a thought to what my feet are doing. This gives my mind a chance to wander as I try to remember the lyrics to some Simon and Garfunkel songs, like "The 59th Street Bridge Song (Feelin' Groovy)," and I think of Art Garfunkel's hike across Europe – apparently, from France to Turkey. I wonder why he didn't answer my email message, and I ponder sending him a message that the book, "Europe, One Step at a Time," is available on Amazon where he would have easy access to a copy.

We are a tiny community – those of us who have walked across Europe. I have joined the likes of Sir Patrick Michael Leigh Fermor, who would become known as a British author, scholar and soldier. He was 18 years old in 1933 when he started his walk the length of Europe, from the Hook of Holland to Constantinople (now Istanbul). In my mind, his accomplishment is tainted by the fact that, toward the end of the trek, he rode a horse for a length of the journey.

Now the Internet mentions another experience described in a book available from Amazon: "Nick Hunt is the author of 'Walking the Woods and the Water: In Patrick Leigh Fermor's Footsteps from the Hook of Holland to Istanbul,' to be published by Nicholas Brealey in Fall 2014, on sale October 28th." I'll want to find that book to compare our experiences.

And I've read online that Peter Jonas, the British opera company director, intended to pursue two lengthy treks: "I want to walk across Europe in both directions – from north to south and east to west, Inverness to Palermo and Warsaw to Lisbon – and I'm determined to do it." I've not learned any more about the plans Peter Jonas was formulating, and I'm curious if his dreams were fulfilled.

Now I'm tired of thinking of the hikes of others and turn my mind to something else entirely. I wonder whether the growth of the grapes and potatoes, which are further along now than they were up north, would seem to be standing still if I had been hiking north instead of southward. Some oddities in my surroundings distract me: in the distance a parachutist is falling from the sky while another robotic lawnmower is obediently clipping every blade of grass beside the house on my left. Then I pass through the community of Halligdorf where a sign indicates the town was 1000 years old in 2006. That's old!

A red-brick wall passing beside me holds a sign with a picture of some wind turbines and with the foreground of a circle with slanted line through it. Words on the sign, *"Keine Zerstörung unserer Heimat"* (no destruction of our home), express opposition to a planned wind farm. An ATV passes me on the road, and I wonder if their use of the roadway isn't against local regulations. Soon after, a one-person egg-shaped car goes by and I ponder when we'll see those in Canada. Then a sign at the far end of a town wishes me well with just one word, *"Tschüss"* (bye).

I have some long hills to climb and, when I check my iPhone for the local temperature, it is 28 degrees and with a 54% humidity. My T-shirt is starting to feel damp when a welcome wind comes up and cools me off. I've come to feel as thirsty as the fields look, and I've been drinking litres of water. I realize that this could deplete my electrolytes (such as potassium and sodium), so I'll need to buy a container of apple juice at the next store. That will hit the spot.

A thirsty walk brings me the 33 kilometres to the community of Hankensbuttel where the hostel is unstaffed. I follow the German instructions on the door, and the manager answers the phone and arrives five minutes later to assign me a room. Not for the first time, I'm alone in a hostel overnight. Before settling in for the evening, I walk the kilometre into town for supper. The restaurant looks old and tired, with unused furnishings in the corners and the smell of ancient dust.

Monday, May 29, 2017

In the morning the family doing housekeeping chores at the hostel appear unhappy with my presence: they don't smile, and they answer my questions brusquely. I seem to be interfering with their preparations for the arrival of a large group. While I eat their meagre breakfast, I think of all those who don't like me – cars think I'm an intrusion; hostels think I should plan better and book ahead; stores think I should know the local shopping habits and not look for things (like prune juice) that are hard to find. I ask myself whether I always like all of them, and I have to admit I don't always. Sometimes I seem to have only one friend, and that friend is McDonald's.

I start out on my hike and pass an unusual decorative feature. Against the red-brick wall of a house – within a side yard of brickwork and shrubbery – someone has built a model two-storey wood chalet with a pair of dwarfs up on its balcony. On the first floor is a wicket where one can get, *"Eier aus Freilandhaltung"* (free range eggs) and *"Kartoffeln"* (potatoes). This is an appealing setting, and the eggs and potatoes must be top quality.

Walking through a community, I see pairs of neighbour women chatting. They have just finished a long weekend that started with Father's Day on Thursday, so there must be many details to cover. I ask them: "Is there a café here?"

"The bakery is 300 metres back. They have coffee there."

I reply, *"Vielen Dank"* (thank you), but decide the cup of coffee will have to wait. I don't want to lengthen the hike more than is necessary.

In the cute, clean village of Knesebeck, I pass a red-brick Lutheran church with a pointed black steeple. It looks simple but attractive, and the doors are open, so I take a look inside. A balcony, that includes the choir loft, makes its way around the walls, and the two ends come close to meeting above the sanctuary. Across from the church is a schoolyard abuzz with activity. A kindergarten group is helping their teacher clean up the yard. The children get to take turns pushing the toy wheelbarrow laden with clippings.

The GPS instructions on my iPhone direct me down a path for a kilometre and then onto a roadway. Well outside of town, I am directed to turn right when, suddenly, everything is the opposite of the cute little village I just left behind.

Now I'm on a road that looks different from others as it leads straight with not a hill or curve in sight. On my left a two-metre-high fence, topped by three strands of razor wire, continues into the distance ahead of me. Then I notice a sign on the fence – a board with a picture of the head of a German shepherd dog and the words, *"Betreten verboten, Vorsicht bissige Hunde"* (Forbidden to enter, careful biting dogs). I am beginning to wonder what is behind that fence: "Is it a motorcycle gang? Is it a rich person's private estate?" A sign indicates that the expanse is private property, so it couldn't be a military base, for example.

Now I notice a few other features. On the other side of the fence on my left are two tracks for vehicles to drive on, then a three-metre-wide length of sand, then shrubbery with razor wire wound throughout and then a forest of mature pine, oak and spruce trees. This pattern will continue for 11 kilometres.

Then I see more oddities. A forest of young oaks on my right has signs warning to stay out because of hidden explosives: *"Lebensgefahr! Absolutes Betretungsverbot"* (Risk of death! Entrance absolutely forbidden). The sun is beating down on this deserted stretch, and all those trees, far from the roadway, cannot provide me with shade. A few signs warn against using flying drones in the area: *"Drohnenüberflug verboten"* (drone flight prohibited).

After I spend an hour trudging along this pattern of road, fence, trees and signs, a vehicle comes into view. It approaches in the distance and passes without incident. The lettering on the white van says something about appliance repair. I feel better in knowing this is a public roadway. Then I'm alone again.

At some point I assume that the forest on my left must be a narrow strip because – through the woods – I can hear cars in the near distance. A road must lie less than a kilometre away on my left. None of this makes sense, and I continue to feel uneasy.

I think of "The Hardy Boys" books of my childhood, with Frank and Joe Hardy solving mysteries and following in the footsteps of their "famous detective" father, Fenton Hardy. I ponder: "If only Frank and Joe were here, they could help me sort out what this is all about."

I now see a break in the pattern far ahead of me. I keep on, under the weight of my backpack and with my hiking poles setting the rhythm, as I notice a distant sign that becomes clearer as I approach.

Finally I'm close enough to recognize the round blue and white sign. It reads *"VW, Prüfgelände Ehra"* (for Volkswagen, testing ground Ehra). To my surprise, the puzzling stretch of land on my left houses a test track for Volkswagen, the German automotive manufacturing company. And I was so worried!

I assume the area on my right is out of bounds as a former military base where ordnance may still lie buried. The experience of these 11 kilometres has been disconcerting, and even seeing the VW sign at the guarded entrance is not comforting. Back home in Canada, Joanne and I are in the process of having the Volkswagen people take back our diesel Golf, one of the fleet in which the VW people cheated on the emissions control systems. The sounds I heard through the trees were vehicles on a test track, so their cheating on the environment and on thousands of customers could have originated at this Volkswagen site. A few cars are entering the front gate of the site, and I wonder what mischief they may now be planning.

The last few days have been as sweaty an experience as any of my days since starting in Portugal ten years ago. Today's temperature is 31 degrees, and the relative humidity is 39%. Once again, I'm concerned about my electrolytes being depleted: at a convenience store, I find some energy drinks that should work. I consume about five litres of liquid on this 43-kilometre stretch to the city of Wolfsburg.

My decision not to book ahead at hostels has two results. On the one hand, I feel free in not having to get to a certain place at a certain time. On the other hand, I am left with anxiety on the availability of a bed. I try to keep this nagging doubt under control, but sometimes it overwhelms me. Some hostels are not staffed in the evening, so guests need to arrive in the afternoon. With that in mind, at five o'clock in the town of Ehra, I phone the hostel in Wolfsburg as I am running late: "I'll be there in two hours. Will there still be someone in reception then?"

I hurry through the complex route into the modern city of Wolfsburg while I put my phone into power-saving mode because of the extent to which I have used it today. I cross the bridge over the Mittellandkanal (in English, the Midland Canal), rush past dignitaries in suits coming out of office buildings and arrive at the hostel door. I needn't have been worried as this place is a large, busy facility, and the reception staff are present till 10:00 pm. I settle into the hostel and drink another half-litre bottle – this time it's green tea with mango. Then I take an unusual step: I swallow a Motrin tablet to decrease the aching in my feet.

Tuesday, May 30, 2017

Although I'm taking a day off today, I still awaken at quarter to six. I join hundreds of young people and their chaperones for breakfast in the boisterous hall.

Then I am given the instructions on the washer and dryer set – another of so many I have encountered in my treks across Europe. At each hostel I need to ask where these appliances are located and how I pay for their use. I gather my clothes – all going into the same load – and hope the equipment isn't too complicated. By now I have seen every type of system and dealt with the odd complexity. In the case of this laundry area, everything works well till I remove the clothes from the dryer and find they are still damp. I purchase another token and give the machine more drying time. At the end all are still damp, so I drape them over the racks in the *Tröcker Raum* (drying room) to finish the job.

Wolfsburg is loud and wet, with a clattering thunderstorm and continuous rain. I borrow an umbrella at the front desk and make my way the half dozen blocks to a business area.

I locate a barbershop, Friseur Milan, and there the young man with a mound of dyed red hair gives me a short haircut, as requested. He shaves the back of my neck, and I ask: "Can you clip the hair in my ears too?" This leads to a ritual I have not heard described by National Geographic. He rubs the inside of my ears with a substance that is flammable, to help burn the hair, or non-flammable, to protect the skin. Then he sets each ear on fire!

He doesn't have a cigarette lighter, so he borrows one from the other man cutting hair. As he lights each ear, it sizzles and smells of scorching. Then he lights it again till he is satisfied or till I convince him that this is becoming painful. Then he runs his finger throughout each ear to remove the ashes. A few days later, I would be taking a selfie of my ears, now with blackened areas, especially on the ear lobes; and, a week or so after this barbecue, my ears look normal again. I have since read that this treatment avoids having these tiny hairs drop into the ear canal when clipped and causing problems there. I don't know; it just seems weird.

I find the city library and, after a frustrating hour of trying to get through to my Gmail account, head for an Internet café. There – to my relief – I access my account immediately, send out "Trek Message 5" and wonder why I have to endure the frustrations that have nothing to do with walking. The hiking itself is usually the simplest part of the trek.

I am told that the city is worth a visit. With its huge auto plant, Wolfsburg is the centre of the Volkswagen enterprise, and residents have the highest average income of any city in Germany. Volkswagen symbolism is everywhere, and even the sections of the hostel are named after Volkswagen models – Jetta, Tiguan and Passat. Areas of the city have to do with the Volkswagen brand, including the Autostadt Volkswagen theme park, and few of the residents' vehicles are non-Volkswagen products.

The science centre, auto museum and art galleries receive high praise from the locals. However, I'm in my usual niche of placing all my energy into the hike and having little interest in distractions. If I arrived by car, bus or train, I would have the vigour to do all this touring. However, I don't and won't.

Fifty years ago my university psychology classes learned of Maslow's "hierarchy of needs." The American psychologist, Abraham Maslow, had developed the idea of the steps of a hierarchy to explain the patterns in human motivation. According to this theory, human motivation moves through five levels of having needs met – from the basic physiological level, through safety, love/belonging and esteem to self-actualization.

In my hiking I am stuck at the first two levels of Maslow's hierarchy – the physiological level of eating and sleeping, as well as the next level of staying safe on the route. As a result, efforts toward love/belonging, esteem or self-actualization are left behind, or – more accurately – do not exist. My energy goes into maintenance of this body and keeping it safe.

According to Maslow, the prerequisite for advancing in the hierarchy is one's fulfillment at the lower levels and the presence of a community in which to develop toward the upper levels. Given the shifting groups around me and my urgency to keep surviving, I'll not be fulfilled at a higher level. I'll enjoy that journey at home. Meanwhile, my irritation with speeding cars shows in my curious mumbling: "Maslow's hierarchy of needs; society's hierarchy of vehicles."

Back at the hostel, supper includes a choice of four kinds of meat, as well as roasted potatoes topped with a dressing of quark and herbs. The young people – from six to sixteen years of age – are as enthusiastic about this meal as I am. It is delicious, and the price is right at a few euros.

Wednesday, May 31, 2017

My last meal at the hostel – an elaborate breakfast of breads, meats and cheeses, yogurt, juice and coffee – prepares me for today's 44 kilometres to the town of Schöningen. Then the first two kilometres include a few wrong turns as I head out of the city. After the opulence of Wolfsburg, I am back onto a simple trail. I enjoy the quiet countryside, visit a gas station café for a cup of coffee and let the sights and sounds of the city move from my awareness to my memory.

At some point on the trail, a rhythmic pounding – like the heartbeat of earth – meets my ears. Here is another mystery to be solved, but the booming now comes with mechanical sounds of metal scraping and clanging. As I round a curve in the road, I recognize the source of the racket as a tall machine pounding guardrail posts into the roadside. I wave at the operator as I pass his deafening equipment.

From the height of a ridge, I appreciate the green quilt spreading into the distance: a series of fields form hues of green framed by woods in emerald and jade. At some point I walk through brambles on the trail and rip a pant leg. I'll need to stitch that upon arrival at the hostel.

When I get to Schöningen, I'm the only guest at the hostel once again. I get a feeling of self-satisfaction in thinking that hostels were meant for hikers like me. Up to 99% of hostel guests arrive by car, and the few of us walking or biking don't even have a car in which to catch some sleep should we find the hostel closed. We are exposed to the world and the weather, and we count on the convenience of the hostel system to comfort us.

As I leave the hostel each day, the GPS on my iPhone takes me from the short streets of a town to the longer roads in the country and back to the maze of small streets as I arrive in a hostel town at day's end. The need to be aware of turns in those streets means constant use of my iPhone and depletion of its battery. I have now been left without power several times, despite use of the "low power mode," and will need to purchase a backup battery at my next opportunity.

Thursday, June 1, 2017

I'm in a pensive mood this morning and realize that my minimal existence lets me see things in more detail and on a new level. The pieces of fresh fruit at breakfast are decorative features that can sustain us both aesthetically and physically.

Then I come to the conclusion that hostels are the sum total of hotel plus activity, light, alcohol, families, kids and games. And I wonder which makes more sense – sitting in a car that zooms by or trudging along the side of the road. So, my hours on the trail remain sessions of musing about any number of unimportant issues.

In my treks across Europe, I've been the only guest at a hostel a few times. I wonder whether there's a rule that hostels need to be open to all at all times. With a few exceptions, this has been my experience: hostellers go out of their way to give me a bed if I happen to be the only guest for the night.

I've seen some pleasant sights this morning. The dining area at the hostel was flowing with sunlight, so I took a photo of it. Now I stop and take a picture of an A-frame house of dark wood that is a Hansel and Gretel cottage surrounded by a perfect landscape of trees, flowers and shrubbery.

I enter the community of Söllingen, and there, on my left in the middle of a sugar beet field, I see a complex steel building with the name "Strübe" in large letters. As I stop and gaze at that structure, a local bus pulls up, and a middle-aged woman gets off. She is nattily dressed and clutches a purse, and – in response to my questions – she explains: "They do research here for the Strübe sugar beet company. I look after the staff cafeteria in the red-brick building on the right. That's where the company offices are."

She continues: "During the Second World War, children would run through the fields here. They would grab a sugar beet, hide it under their coat and run home. They were so hungry that they would chew pieces and it would give them some vegetables and sugar." And, again, I am dismayed at the need for me to experience the horrors of war – in this case, the starving children of Germany – as I hike through this peaceful land. At 70 years of age and having heard a lifetime of war stories, mainly about my native Netherlands, I still can't make any sense of that needless suffering.

The woman also becomes one of several people to tell me about a railroad halfway up a hill in the distance. She says I'm headed toward the area and suggests the restored train with its steam locomotive would be worth a ride. This joins the suggestion from others that I visit the famous botanical garden that must be halfway up the same mountain. I think I'll let it all go by: I'm busy, and it's uphill!

As we stand their chatting, another woman comes out of the Strübe office building and has a list of people who have ordered lunch for that day. They have a little chat, and I realize I am cutting into the workday, so I thank the cafeteria lady and hike away.

I've seen a few people walking lately, though none had backpacks. Theirs seem to be local strolls while I'm headed toward the ridge of hills in the distance. Meanwhile I'm now filling the hours with trying to recall the lyrics to songs of the traditional Dutch variety. Many refrains – such as that of *"Daar bij die molen"* (there by that windmill) – come easily, but words to the verses lie somewhere between challenging and impossible to recall.

I hike through some pretty communities, including Jerxheim, and pass a tiny roadside park with bench, stone marker and sign, which reads: *"Hier waren Deutschland und Europa bis zum 8. Dezember 1989 um 12 Uhr geteilt."* (Here Germany and Europe were divided until December 8, 1989 at 12 o'clock.) On this spot the official ceremony was held to recognize the re-unification of East and West Germany. I imagine dignitaries in their finery, reporters with their notebooks and, perhaps, a band playing a German marching tune. Now all that remains of that activity is this isolated park with bench, marker and sign.

Here I enter old East Germany and immediately notice differences from old West Germany. Now one-lane concrete roads run through farmland. The concrete is actually laid in two sections – for the right and left vehicle wheels – and these would have led to a collection of a dozen barns and an apartment building that was part of the communist agricultural collectivization program. Now most of the farm buildings are gone, but these side roads remain as a testament to a piece of German history. As I write about this in my notebook, a deer bounds across the trail ahead of me and reminds me that nature can survive all political schemes.

The route on my iPhone takes me down one of these two-section roadways through fields of grain to an unknown destination. The concrete surfaces run in a straight line, but they never start or end in a village. Rather, they connect two vague points on rural roads, and I have faith in GPS to help me find my way along a reasonably direct path southward.

In fact, I have come to trust my iPhone more than I trust people in giving me information on which way to go. When I ask local folks for details about turning at a remote intersection, they seem uncertain as they have not hiked the route themselves. More frustrating are those times when people convince me they are sure of the path, but kilometres later I discover their suggestions were incorrect and led me astray.

I pass alternating wheat and sugar beet fields and enter a village where two men in a pick-up truck stop out of curiosity at my appearance as a long-distance hiker. Both speak limited English, but we have a reasonable conversation. The driver owns a nearby farm – one I admired as I passed – and he says: "I grow wheat, sugar beets and *Raps*." Thanks to former Canadian Prime Minister, John Diefenbaker, I could understand that *Raps* was similar to the English word "rapeseed," which is now called "canola" in Canada.

At some point in the late 1950's or early 1960's, as either Progressive Conservative leader or Prime Minister, Diefenbaker spoke in Parliament in support of the rape of Canadian Prairie farmers. This got a chuckle, mainly from Diefenbaker himself, and he immediately clarified that he was referring to the rapeseed grown in his constituency of Prince Albert, Saskatchewan. Since that time and, perhaps, to salvage its image, this seed grain has been renamed "canola," standing for a contraction of "Canada" and "ola," meaning oil.

As I continue my hike, I think back on Henry in the city of Mérida, southern Spain. There I ended up at a little hotel where I met this German man at breakfast. Henry had previously hiked through the area on the Via de la Plata pilgrimage route and came back to take a closer look at the city's archaeological features. Now I think of returning to some of my favourite places across Europe. I've seen so much in the 11 countries that it would be hard to choose a favourite place to visit and to share with Joanne.

I am brought to the reality of a steep slope upward by a sign indicating a 10% rise. It certainly feels like it, and I eventually make it to the town of Wernigerode after a 45-kilometre day, most of which was spent avoiding passing cars and speeding tractors as I hugged a narrow shoulder.

Surprisingly, today I headed westward in travelling from "West" to "East." This morning I started in Schöningen in old West Germany, travelled in a southwesterly direction and ended up in Wernigerode in old East Germany. The boundary line curves back and forth, and – as with so many borders on my hikes – this one has its peculiarities.

With its cream stucco exterior and dark roof with dormers, the Wernigerode hostel looks like a chateau of old. Unfortunately, the music facility that takes up much of its space is humming, and all beds are taken by the visiting students. I was advised to get a room at the Hasseröder Burghotel, a nine-storey modern structure of white and grey concrete a few blocks away. I enjoyed the classy features of this hotel and my view of treed hillsides and red roofs. However, I found it awfully quiet and missed the buzz of the group in the hostel.

Some hotels ask to see my passport when I check in, and the Hasseröder Burghotel is one of these. On the one hand, wearing the passport in its belt under my clothing becomes a chore. On the other hand, I'm pleased that someone developed a system for sailors in olden days to "pass" out of the "port" into the neighbouring community to visit. In the modern age, I've been allowed to leave the airport at Aalborg, Denmark and to enter – and travel throughout – the European Community.

In a text message, Joanne mentions Valdy, the Canadian folk and country musician from the early 1970's. He is known for "Rock N Roll Song" ("I came into town as a man of renown, a writer of songs about freedom and joy . . ."). Valdy will be performing at Shepody House, the music venue in a repurposed Baptist church in our local village of Dorchester, New Brunswick. While in the area, he will spend one night at the Airbnb in our home, and I feel bad in missing out. It would have been a thrill to chat with the person representing radio favourites of my past.

In my response to Joanne's message, I mention a few details about my life on the trail. My iPhone has only a bit of power left while I'm texting, which I find disconcerting as I need the phone to tell both Joanne and me where I'm located. Later I add another note: "The hostel had no room, but a nearby hotel did – with free ticket to a sauna-swim facility a block away and a free drink at the bar, where I am now. Forget hostels!"

Friday, June 2, 2017

Before leaving Wernigerode I visit a "Vodaphone Business Store" that I happen to pass. A German message on my iPhone seems to read that my service will end within 24 hours. The store clerk, Tobias, explains: "The system needs proof of your identity. Otherwise, your service will stop." Thankfully, Tobias simply has to look at my passport and input the information. I've just learned another lesson: if I were to start in Germany again, I should get the SIM card at a Vodaphone shop, not at a grocery store. I need shop staff who are familiar with the intricacies applying to a cross-country hiker. Of course, I have no intention of a third hike through Germany. Twice is enough!

Tobias is young enough that his scraggly beard is trying to decide which way to turn. He's a talkative lad: "I'm interested in Canada because my father worked in the woods there. He said they had to hang food from tree limbs so the bears wouldn't eat it."

Then he describes a tourist attraction I'll see on a distant hill: "On your left after you leave Wernigerode, you can see the remains of an ancient castle. It's worth a visit." I appreciate the stories Tobias shares and his concern for my iPhone issues.

Leaving the Vodaphone shop, I stroll through the town centre, past shops with walls of red bricks and wooden beams. In the country outside of Wernigerode, I catch sight of the remains of the crumbling sandstone edifice that Tobias mentioned. Again, I decide not to be a tourist taking a detour to this landmark as I still have a chunk of Europe to cover. Instead, I take a photo that shows the crumbling building as a dim distant feature and that doesn't do it justice, I'm sure.

I hike through a natural area of woods and marsh that shows little evidence of this being old East Germany. Historical peculiarities do not show up in nature but, rather, in the things people created, such as concrete country lanes, isolated apartment buildings and crumbling sidewalks thick with weeds. The infrastructure tells obvious differences between East and West, whereas the natural world doesn't recognize political boundaries. On my left now, the *Autobahn* streams with traffic, erasing the boundary between old East and West Germany, while a peaceful stretch of deciduous woods stretches ahead of me on my right.

Beside my bicycle path along a smaller highway, I come upon a gadget to catch speeders. It's on a tripod and surrounded by camouflage material so as not to be visible from a distance. I toy with the idea of warning drivers of its presence, but that would be complicated – and, no doubt, illegal – so I hurry on my way.

I arrive in the town of Thale and stop at a roadside construction project. Cement is being poured as the ground floor of a new building. The material comes out of a mixer truck through a hose in a metal frame that goes upward and then down to a nozzle to be spread as a new floor. And I think of my late brothers, John and Tony, who were in the concrete floor finishing business. They would have appreciated this technology over the old parade of wheelbarrows being filled from a cement mixer truck, pushed over wire mesh to be dumped and taken back to the truck to be refilled. In my younger day, the continuous round of wheelbarrows would remind me of an amusement park's carousel.

I head for the hostel, but it is closed in preparation for a big event the next day, so the staff suggest a nearby hotel. This is the Hotel Schloss, and – with its dark corners and creaky doors – it reminds me of the Munsters television program. Unfortunately, the Hotel Schloss has no vacancy, but I sit in the manager's office while she uses the phone to find me a bed for the night.

I keep being surprised at the degree to which lodging of all kinds is in high use throughout Europe. This time a bed is found a few kilometres away – at the end of a 36-kilometre day – in the next village of Bad Suderode. "The next village," sounds ominous and might require another hour or two of walking. In fact, it is only a few kilometres, and I end up in the Kurhotel with its well-dressed clientele who, obviously, are not here with backpacks.

Earlier in history this must have been an area of health resorts, seeing that the names of so many towns include the word *"Bad"* (bath). The village of Bad Suderode features one of several spas in the area, and the local spring water is noted for its exceptionally high concentration of calcium.

I go to the hotel's patio café and order a small beer. I'm interested in their soup and salad, and I wait for someone to take my order. And I wait and wait and wait. The server is socializing with other clients and finally passes my table. I ask if he can take my order, and he says: "I was waiting for your wife to arrive." I assure him that Joanne is back in Canada and won't be dining with me today.

Then the food preparation takes a while, and – exactly an hour after I sit down – the soup and salad find their way to my table. After enduring a full day's hike, being sent from place to place for a bed and being tested by a waiter, I feel as though I'm losing a bit of contact with reality. Or, I should say, it's losing contact with me as things are becoming more absurd. I feel that I'm toughening up physically and can handle any obstacle to my continuous hike, but this may come at the price of mental stability.

On my way from the patio dining area to my room, I pass the vacated reception desk in disappointment. I planned to get the Wi-Fi password, but the receptionist has already left for the day. I go back to ask the waiter for the password, but he says he cannot get it for me. I'm perturbed because he should be able to give me the password – something that must be readily available – and, besides, if he hadn't taken an hour to feed me, I could have caught the receptionist before she went home. I guess I'll have to use the limited data I bought for my iPhone.

On my trek the important thing about each room is not its degree of luxury but whether it comes with a heater so I can dry my clothes. Sometimes I need to dry my poncho, before putting it back in its pouch, if it's wet with rain. And, of course, there's always a hand wash to be done. Now I'm fortunate to have a drying area since my hotel room features a balcony, which – unfortunately – I can't use because it's raining. The soil has been dry, so farmers must be happy with this gift from the heavens even if I'm not.

Saturday, June 3, 2017

In the morning I go to the reception desk to get the Wi-Fi password so I can use some free data before breakfast. The receptionist informs me they have a complex system for providing passwords. It requires an electronically produced code for each guest, and only the receptionist can access these. I immediately half-forgive last evening's waiter. He was right about the password restrictions, but he could have been quicker with his service.

Breakfast this morning is the most extensive I've seen, with 50 or so items to choose from – breads, cereal, cheeses, meats, preserves, fruit preparations and yogurt. There are also a few salads: perhaps these serve as a nod to visitors from Poland where salads are a breakfast staple. The size of this spread matches the cost of the room.

As I leave Bad Suderode, a warm drizzle starts, so it's time put on my poncho, and soon I'm perspiring under its plasticized fabric. Despite that irritation – or because of it – I feel strong. I'm now climbing the steep hills that glaciers left behind eons ago. I feel as though, way back then, nature was already conspiring against me. Between all those hills, the Internet can be unpredictable, leaving me guessing at the route I should take.

Every kilometre or two, I see a tower serving as hunting blind. Each of these is a simple cabin of wood with a ladder leading up to its door – certainly, more than a platform in a tree. I cross a railway track that is of an unusually narrow gauge, perhaps a remnant of communist days. On the approach to the town of Harzgerode, hills block Internet reception, and I use my paper map as backup.

At a grocery store, I purchase two green items – a package of watermelon slices, with their rinds upward, and a "green smoothie," which consists of matcha (green tea powder), ginger, kale, pear, spinach, banana and apple. Together, these two things quench my thirst and leave me feeling satisfied. This is another one of those stores with a cafeteria of upholstered chairs, decorative plants and pleasant artwork that make you want to take some time to relax. I wonder if fellow customers may be saying to each other: "Oh, that's the guy hiking from Denmark that we've heard so much about." But I doubt it as no one asks for an autograph.

After Harzgerode the GPS takes me on a paved bike path, but it ends in a field of weeds. I hike straight ahead through about 200 metres of nettles burning my bare legs when I suddenly find myself on a new road atop a dam at the edge of a lake. The changes in hiking trails can be astounding, and here I went from the ease of a bicycle path, through the frustration of a field of nettles to the peace of a lake behind a natural stone dam – all that over a few hundred metres.

You can't predict what's coming next: this time it's a one-kilometre road of rounded rocks that are so hard on the soft soles of my feet after all those kilometres of hiking. These stones seem to be a holdover from the days when this state of Saxony-Anhalt was part of communist East Germany. I experienced similar surfaces on my first trek through old East Germany five years ago.

As I saw on that trek through former communist areas, I now come across a deserted white brick apartment building. It has broken windows and is located away from any

103

community. This would have been housing for the people assigned to the farm collectivization program, which placed groups of families out in the country to support agricultural operations. Now many of these vacated apartment buildings are wondering about their fate.

Under the shelter of a tall highway overpass, I phone ahead to the next hostel, and a friendly voice answers that they have room for me. After a long day's hike, I arrive in the town of Kelbra at 8:00 pm and share the small hostel with a young couple and four families. The young man whom I had phoned is the only staff on duty, and he covers the reception desk, the bar area and anything else that needs doing. It's late, no restaurant is nearby and I'm tired. To my dismay I'm grouchy and short with the young man, answering his questions abruptly and grumbling as I fill out another registration form.

On his part, he remains friendly and upbeat as he books me into a room. With his help I make a supper menu out of things available at the hostel bar – a glass of dark beer and a cylinder of Pringle "cheese and onion" chips. Now I feel better, and we have a brief chat about the hostel, which he says will be busier in the summer, while he is interrupted by questions from other guests. He remains friendly throughout, and I make a mental note to work at being nicer to people at the end of each tiring day.

Today's guests are a mixed lot of adults and children, and I think that I must stand out as coming from Canada, being all alone and having hiked 47 kilometres today. Again, I'm caught between the joy of staying anonymous – not having to answer to anyone – and the wish to shout out: "Do you know what I did today?" And all the guests might turn to me with a sense of wonder or, perhaps, with the thought that it just sounds silly. In each hostel I have that urge as I seem to be the only one who is serious about the hostel ideal of lengthy hikes through nature.

In the hostel's upper floor, I see half a dozen children playing a form of ping-pong where they walk around the table while hitting the ball back and forth. This is a game our children have enjoyed from time to time. And I thought it was our invention!

JOSEPH KOOT

4. Southern Germany

Sunday, June 4, 2017

Soon after setting out this morning, I'll be leaving the more northerly German state of Saxony-Anhalt and entering a more southerly state of Thuringia. This boundary is unmarked and unremarkable, so I can only guess where the transition lies.

At some point, my iPhone instantly reacts to an Internet signal. I'm surprised at this speed of response till I realize I'm standing right under a cell tower. Out here deep in countryside, my GPS instructions tell me to take small paved roads that serve as shortcuts between highways.

Over the last few days, swallows have been flying low because of the rain. And I recall a children's magazine from my youth – the Catholic "Treasure Chest," which came to us from the USA. It explained that bugs fly at a decreased altitude in response to the low-pressure area that comes with unsettled weather. Then birds hover lower to catch those bugs in their open beaks. This behaviour doesn't seem to have changed in the intervening years or between North America and Europe.

As I pass through the community of Ichstedt, the snout of one dog after another appears under the gates on my left, close to my ankles, as they bark and yelp and long for blood.

107

Then on my right, a woman honks when I'm not quick enough in crossing the yield lane at an intersection while a young boy in the passenger seat stares at this strange backpacked image.

My hikes in spring have coincided with European holidays. Today is another of those: it is *Pfingsten* (Pentecost), the Christian feast celebrating the descent of the Holy Spirit on the disciples of Jesus. This holy day is celebrated 50 days after Easter and 10 days after the Ascension of Jesus into Heaven. Celebrations continue from Sunday into Monday, so tomorrow will be another day of closed shops.

In the community of Ringleben, a restaurant appears to be open and advertises *Spargel mit Erdbeeren* (white asparagus with strawberries) as a sidekick to ice cream and with a topping of whipped cream. So that becomes my dessert after a main course of potatoes with pork slices. As was my experience on the previous trek going from west to east through Germany, the bitterness of the *Spargel* refuses to disappear despite the sweetness of the other ingredients.

The path I'm walking continues to fascinate. A gecko poses on the sidewalk ahead of me, and I reach for my iPhone, but it scurries away before I can capture its fleeting image. Then, in the middle of farm country, the trail's surface includes round storm drain covers, which normally appear only in built up areas back home. I realize that these features must indicate a past of collective farms with their accompanying apartment complexes from communist days – a past that is now only memories and storm drain lids.

After 27 kilometres I arrive in the town of Heldrungen and look forward to a hostel bed in a castle that is advertised as featuring its original moat. The setting looks as interesting as I had assumed, but the number of teens and adults forewarn me that there is no room for me at the castle. The apologetic woman in reception suggests, "You might try the home of Veronika Weber," and she draws a map on a paper napkin.

I find my way down the few blocks to this possible guesthouse and knock, but no one answers. A woman passes the house pushing a child in her stroller, and I ask: "Do you know Veronika Weber? Where could I find her?" In the way of small towns, this woman not only knows Veronika but is, in fact, her daughter.

She says: "My mother is with my sister across the street. I was just going to visit them." I follow her to the sister's house where Veronika decides I can stay in the guesthouse, but I have to come back in an hour. From the hesitant translation of one of the daughters, I understand that the young women question why I can't just stay now, but their mother insists the lodging needs tidying first.

This being the feast of *Pfingsten*, the few eateries in town are closed, but I saw a barbecue special advertised at the *Rathaus* (town hall) a few blocks back, so that is where I head. A middle-aged couple owns the "Chaise Lounge" bar in a wing of the *Rathaus*, and today's offering consists of sausages right from the smoking barbecue in the yard. They are also serving beer, potato salad and waffles, and this becomes my supper and dessert. The owners of the café speak a smattering of English between them, and the odd customer drops by to sneak a look at this odd English-speaking Canadian.

It occurs to me that this is a good place to round out my information about the days of Communism in old East Germany. It might be worthwhile to satisfy my curiosity, to get historical details for this book and to connect with the local people on a deeper level. However, I can't bring myself to go beyond the daily narrative of my hike into their memories of a time that lay outside my experience. As a visitor – and not a reporter – I can't connect with them and don't want to intrude. So, I let historical peculiarities lie and, instead, speak of my hike and their café.

At my home for the night, I show Veronika pictures of our Airbnb back in Canada, and she asks how much we charge. Our fee is $70 per night; hers is 25 Euros (about 40 Canadian dollars). I guess from her raised eyebrows that she thinks she should charge more. Then she leaves, and I'm alone in this spotless house. Each street in old East Germany seems to be a combination of dilapidated buildings and renovated ones. Among those, Veronika's home has been perfectly restored.

Monday, June 5, 2017

Yesterday I bought a few extra waffles at the *Rathaus* eatery where they were being sold as dessert. Those now serve as my breakfast along with the rest of a carton of juice. I wonder: "After my departure will Veronika be sharing stories about me with the couple who run the bar at the *Rathaus*?" She is aware of our Airbnb venture at home; they were left with details about my hiking. Perhaps they'll put the anecdotes together into a local legend.

On this holiday Monday celebrating *Pfingsten*, the only shops that are open are the gas stations. Each of those has a café with a dozen stools and good coffee even if it comes out of a machine. I welcome both the coffee and the chance to take off my backpack and hiking boots.

For a few days, hills are more plentiful, and short stretches of flat road are a pleasant break between the ups and downs. Among the hills I see sections of a narrow-gauge railway, and fields with crops are now interspersed with fruit orchards. Hilly stretches come with natural areas that are filled with birdsong – chirps, cheeps, coos and cuckoos. The birds must feed on the black insects that consider my eyes and ears their passing banquet. Here nature attracts visitors who are absorbed in specific features. These tourists approach things and inspect them while I glance at things as they pass.

A roadside panel with tourism information shows a map with 450 kilometres of bicycle paths around a series of lakes. Many people are enjoying a holiday outing when a rainstorm erupts and cycling families head for shelter. As quickly as possible, I go through the process of taking off my backpack, getting out my rain poncho, putting on my backpack and throwing the poncho back over my head so it covers my backpack and me. In a sudden storm, this can leave me damp for the day.

This proves to be a long day of 51 kilometres, and the rain stops as I enter Erfurt. This city is halfway along my 1,000-kilometre hike down the length of Germany, from Flensburg in the north to the Austrian border at Salzburg in the south. At first sight Erfurt is a dull city, but one redeeming item, appearing along the sidewalk, is a lime green and glass cubicle. It looks like a telephone booth but has a few shelves with books to read and a book-shaped bench outside the glass compartment. The words "Open Book" appear on top of the structure, and this mini-library looks truly inviting.

A few blocks further, I find the hostel, which is an older model with four soaring stone pillars in front of a balconied entranceway. Its aged appearance reflects the lack of modern services: to my dismay, it has no washer and dryer, which I had planned to use on tomorrow's day off. This edifice is hosting a group of special needs teens, so the complex role of hostels continues.

Tuesday, June 6, 2017

With the lack of services at the hostel, I walk through sections of Erfurt to track down a laundry facility and an Internet café where I can type "Trek Message 6." My route takes me down Juri-Gagarin-Ring, a street named for the famed cosmonaut, Yuri Alekseyevich Gagarin. He was a Soviet pilot and the first human to journey into outer space when his Vostok spacecraft completed an orbit of the Earth on April 12, 1961. Then I walk through Karl-Marx-Platz, named for the German philosopher and revolutionary socialist, Karl Marx. He published "The Communist Manifesto" and "Das Kapital," anti-capitalist works that form the basis of Marxism. Both Yuri Gagarin and Karl Marx were important personages for communist regimes, such as that of old East Germany. I find this fascinating: here communism is gone, but those names remain.

In Erfurt's central square, eight pairs of tram tracks (so, 16 rails) crisscross the brickwork at various angles. Pedestrians and cyclists adapt to trams coming at them from all directions, and I cross a number of those tracks on my way to the nearest commercial laundry, a half hour's walk away. When I get there, it's no longer a laundry but is in the process of converting into a different business. Eventually I find a laundry service on my way back to the hostel.

At a fancy outdoor café, Kirsten brings me the white asparagus soup I ordered. She isn't busy and asks: "Why are you visiting Erfurt?"

I respond: "I'm hiking south from northern Denmark. My path is taking me through Erfurt here. When I finish the next part north from southern Greece, I plan to write another book about the journey."

She is interested in getting a copy of my book about the previous trek of 6,000 kilometres from Portugal to Estonia, and I suggest: "Just look in Amazon for the eBook edition. That would be the simplest way to read my story." Europeans keep being interested in my wish to hike across their continent, and they often seem intrigued that it is not a fellow European doing so.

My hiking usually doesn't leave energy or interest for visiting art displays. However, several churches in Erfurt grab my attention, starting with *Predigerkirche* (Preacher's Church). This edifice had been built as the monastic sanctuary of the local Dominican friary in the 13th century when the mystic Meister Eckhart was prior here. This Catholic place of worship became a Protestant church after the Reformation, so its interior shows the uplifting spirit of the Catholic churches of the Middle Ages rather than the later Protestant dourness.

A short walk away is Wigbertikirche (St. Wigbert's Catholic Church), a late Gothic structure. As I enter, a man is leading a group of high school students down its centre aisle and describing the stained glass windows in this recently renovated building. I meander through the church and happen to meet that tour guide outside. Frank introduces himself as a devotee of local history, and he talks to me about the windows: "An artist from Bavaria designed them. They give us newer ideas about faith."

Traditionally stained glass taught lessons from the Bible and Catholic tradition through the use of colourful pictures. Now these windows use geometric designs in muted colours to reflect the new cosmology and a more universal approach to the miracle of life. A series of rectangles, arrows and spirals tells the story of God's place in the universe and our appreciation of creation.

Frank adds: "Half of the churches in Erfurt are Catholic and half are Lutheran." This ratio has changed as I hiked from the northern border of Germany southward – the north having few Catholic churches, and more of them appearing as I continue southward.

I'm surprised that I see and hear no mention of the close connection of this city with Martin Luther, the leader of the German Reformation. Luther studied philosophy and legal sciences at the University of Erfurt and began his theological education here at St. Augustine's Monastery in 1505. As a monk, he was ordained to the priesthood in 1507 at Erfurt's Cathedral of St. Marien. In the following year, Luther left Erfurt when assigned to the University of Wittenberg to teach theology, and there his subservience became defiance in questioning Catholic Church doctrine.

I keep being amused by my experiences in hostels. Here in Erfurt I was delighted to be the only occupant of a six-bunk room when I arrived; then someone else shows up, and I'm glad to have company. It's fascinating how much inconvenience I feel comfortable accepting on this trek. If Joanne were along, I would be much fussier on the sleeping arrangements and, of course, the length of daily hikes. The choices a couple makes are often far removed from the decisions of each of the two individuals.

The *Speishalle* (dining room) has a sombre atmosphere with half a dozen adults having supper. Then 30 teenagers enter – bringing with them the exuberance of youth – and our supper becomes much more enjoyable. Sometimes the rapid German conversation sounds as though it is mispronounced English, and from another table I misunderstand someone to say, "Turn my tires into spaghetti," which makes no sense at all. Now I'm sure I've been away from the English language for too long.

In late afternoon I return to the laundry facility to pick up my refreshed clothes. On the hike back to the hostel for supper, a sudden shower catches me, and I find cover in a bus shelter. Many people are waiting for the bus, and I feel guilty taking one of their spots. It's curious that I can hike across Europe and be kept dry by my rain poncho but forget it at the hostel when I need it most.

Wednesday, June 7, 2017

My hike across Germany reminds me of things I'd learned on my previous walk through this country: in hostels everyone says, *"Guten Morgen"* (Good morning), to everyone else, and tiny ice cream cones are provided for filling with jam at *Frühstück* (breakfast). You take these back to your table to smear the preserve on your hearty grain-filled bread. I continue to load up my body's furnace at breakfast, and today's hike of 42 kilometres to the town of Ilmenau will take care of any extra calories I consume.

Heading out of Erfurt, I take a picture of a scene that mimics our part of New Brunswick, Canada. The trees, hills and winding road – repaired with patches of pavement – remind me of my home so far away. This area could be a series of parks, and my busy mind pictures two parks of significance during my first trek: one was miserable; the other, delightful.

Early on, a park in the town of Aljustrel, Portugal was the site of my being assaulted by a gang who took my stuff and left me bloody and bruised. Then a park in the city of Szczecin, Poland was the site where a young man in a wheelchair made me realize I was hiking for those who could not, including my late brother Bill. For some reason, fate seems to have chosen me to endure this irrational pursuit.

Back in northern Denmark after the first week of this trek, I felt as though I had gone from first to second gear. Then the walking became easier about halfway down Denmark's expanse when I went from second to third gear. Now the hiking is becoming automatic as I go from third to fourth gear at the point where it seems easier to walk than to stop.

I pass a sign pointing toward a bike path, and its post displays the stylized blue and yellow shell of Spain's pilgrimage routes. In my solo struggle, it feels comforting to be reminded of my hike as one of a crowd moving along Spain's main pilgrimage route, the Camino Francés, eight years and about 6,000 kilometres back. I see no further decals of this nature, so – again – this may simply be a local wish: someone would like to have such a trail, but it hasn't been supported by public funding.

The road has become my life to the point that I feel I own it: I'm involved in every step I take while others zoom by. As visitors, they are not part of my roadside culture. Since the road is my community, I don't feel intrusive in observing the local people I meet though I feel uncomfortable probing too deeply into their personal experiences.

Here communism brought a different way of life than I had seen further north. There in old West Germany, construction was mechanized, and big machines were everywhere. Here in old East Germany, much of the labour requires shovels and wheelbarrows. Then I pass a series of mansions, like those back in the province of Drenthe in the Netherlands, and this brings another insight. A simpler lifestyle doesn't necessarily mean that all members of the community are poor. I assume those living in mansions under communism were far from penniless.

As I walk into strong gusts from the south, a truck flies by and the wind blows my hat into the roadside greenery. I place it on my head more firmly, and moments later I stop to take in an unusual sight. As I cross an overpass, I realize that in one photo frame I can incorporate the junction of two four-lane highways (*Autobahnen* A71 and A4), a high-speed train track and several smaller roads – all of these coming together at one point. The traffic flowing in all directions is dizzying.

As I walk through the village of Ichtershausen, a few shops hug the sidewalk at my right elbow. One is a restaurant in a salmon-coloured stucco building and is called "Indien Aroma." It shows a sketch of an Indian temple on one window and, on the other, an advertising of, *"Geniessen Sie unser internationale Küche"* (enjoy our international cuisine) and *"Herzlich Wilkommen"* (a warm welcome). The doorstep, the windows and – even – the little garbage can/ashtray are polished, and I can't help but enter for lunch.

The middle-aged couple who own the place were originally from the Punjabi region of India. The woman speaks little English and puts her energy into creating richly flavoured Punjabi cuisine. The man lights an incense taper in a burner on a small corner table and takes my order. He is an easy conversationalist and mentions, "When I was younger, I worked in Canada as an electrical consultant in London and

Toronto" – Ontario cities with which I am familiar. The aromas coming from the kitchen leave me famished, and I'm delighted when he brings me the lamb in curry sauce, basmati rice and chai coffee.

The university-age son is doing odd chores, and I am intrigued by the fact that the father, as a Sikh, wears a turban, but the son does not. At moments like this, I – again – wish I were a reporter so I could ask about the men's choices in this matter. However, not wanting to pry, I leave the question unasked and go to the washroom before continuing on my way. As I expected, the toilet area is spotless, with little homey touches of Punjabi art.

Before leaving, I ask about the massive tan-coloured brick building across the street. This edifice is crisscrossed with latticework of dark wood and may have as many as 100 windows lighting its interior. I'm told it had been a factory, the *Thüringische Nadelwerke*, where sewing needles of all kinds were made until it closed a few years ago. Now it serves as symbol of a once-active industry.

In the distance to the south – just where I am headed – loom the Thuringian mountains. The local people are quick to point out that those will be a challenge for me. I would like to challenge them to keep the bad news to themselves!

The west side of the town of Arnstadt is a budding industrial complex, with cranes adding still more buildings. In Arnstadt's downtown a community celebration is taking place. I stop to enjoy the talents of an older man who plays guitar and drums while singing tunes that make the crowd snicker but leave me wishing I knew more German so I could chuckle along.

I've reached a few more milestones: my first booklet of notes is full, my first travel bottle of contact lens solution is empty and I've used up a tube of sunscreen on face, arms and legs. Now my hike takes me down a long country road that leads right into Ilmenau.

The man in reception at the hostel in Ilmenau recommends supper at "Easy Way." However, this bistro is disappointing at every turn. The waitress recommends their Captain Morgan rum-flavoured beer, which proves indecisive in being rum or beer. The spare ribs provide my grease intake for a week and include a hunk of gristle for good measure. Only three of us are dining this evening, and yet the waitress chooses to put me at a table next to that of two women who carry on an animated conversation in competition with the music blaring from the sound system. The personality of the waitress does not compensate for the deficiencies: she is standoffish and disappears for lengthy periods. All in all, this may be the most disappointing meal on either European trek.

Thursday, June 8, 2017

As I leave Ilmenau, hilly terrain lies ahead of me, and the weather is unsettled: it vacillates between clear sky and rain. I'm soon surrounded by the hills of the *Thüringer Wald* (Thuringian Forest) and feel a sense of relief. I had a cold before leaving home on this trek and wondered whether hills would leave me short of breath. As it turns out, I feel comfortable on this hike and continue in the pace I set when I came to my first hills way back in Portugal. I mount hills slowly to avoid my "touch of asthma" from kicking in; then I speed down the other side.

Over a few days, the skin's surface on the right side of my right lower calf has felt irritated. Placing a piece of felt between my leg and my sock has helped. The skin on my leg looks normal, so I don't know what the problem is. I'm just pleased that the issue is resolving itself.

I am now well into the *Thüringer Wald*, and these hills prove to be a treat with flowers – including lupines – filling the glades and with rivulets tumbling down the steeper spots. I think of the changes in my body during my hike from northern Denmark to this point. The scenery outside of me reflects the activity inside: as the water in a river changes constantly, so the cells of my body are a whole new set by the end of another part of my European trek. And I wonder if those cells change more quickly through all this activity than they do in my quieter life at home.

A mixture of deciduous and evergreen trees looms over me, and I enter an area of spruce trees that tower from slopes below me to well above my head. With that height, they must be an old-growth forest, one that has aged without being disturbed. It has the feel of a natural community, not a lumbering enterprise.

Then the wind rises and sounds like rushing water as it races through the treetops. A fence along the road keeps animals from being hit by passing cars, and I notice a wooden crate on a stand with a slot along the bottom. This unit is marked *"Streugut"* (grit) and serves to get cars moving when stuck in icy conditions during winter in this hilly area. Now, early in the tourist season, there are few vehicles; but I'm told there will be car after car going through this pleasant setting in the summer months. Between the hills my cell phone reception becomes sporadic.

As I round another hill, I find myself in the pretty town of Neustadt with its well-tended houses of dark grey, orange and white. The young man in the tourist office is just closing for lunchtime, so he walks with me to answer a few of my questions, "What are those diamond-shaped half-metre wide sheets on the houses?" and "Where could I get some lunch?"

He explains: "During communist times the houses had sidings of asbestos. That is now being replaced with more expensive *Schiefer* [slate]. The winters are bad here, and the slate protects the houses."

He surprises me with an interesting tidbit, "Some of the slate is imported from Canada," and I didn't even know we exported the stuff.

Then we pass one of the two local restaurants, and he recommends it, so I enter while he hurries home for lunch. In this fancy bistro, I enjoy the *solienka* soup from a Russian recipe, as well as a fresh salad and coffee. An elderly couple at the next table ask about my backpack, and I would like to have regaled them with tales of my adventures. However, they speak no English, and my German is basic enough that I didn't so much soar through a speech about my exploits as stumble from word to word. Upon entering an establishment, I'm just another customer. Then they hear my story, and I'm not just another customer after all.

In this restaurant again, I'm faced with the issue of tipping the wait staff. I give a small tip when I receive exceptional service as that seems to be the European custom. Then I feel bad about not giving more, but my guilt is assuaged by the fact that I don't just eat. Rather, I provide staff and customers with unexpected entertainment. So, their restaurant tips and mine balance out: they serve food, I serve fascination.

A few doors down, a church is open, and I venture inside. It's a simple structure in which the main feature is the double balcony all around the area of the assembly. I have often seen balconies in churches, but this is the first time I've seen one balcony hover above the other. I assume this design is meant to add seating capacity to a church that was given a small footprint as a heat-saving feature.

As I hike out of Neustadt, wind gusts arise and – just as quickly – lessen to become a pleasant breeze. I pass a kilometre of trees and come upon a meadow of Queen Anne's lace and buttercups; this pattern repeats with stretches of trees dividing these meadows.

This tranquil scene brings me to be reflective about my situation. I am stuck in a pattern of going from hostel to hostel when it would be nice to be home. There I could be comfortable in not having to find Internet cafés for typing my trek messages and in not having to adapt to various cultures and unfamiliar activities. Now the next hostel awaits me in Schnett, a hamlet so small it doesn't even appear on my map of Germany. After a 28-kilometre day, I climb toward this rustic set of buildings at the top of an unending hill.

When I arrive at the hostel, a man is visiting in the reception area. When I start speaking my basic German, this man says in English, "You must be Dutch," as – in those few words – I had already sounded like someone who speaks Dutch and tries to make it into German. Then he goes on to translate for the hosteller who wishes he could join in but had been taught Russian – and not English – as the second language during those communist days of old East Germany.

The hostel staff are a warm elderly couple who take in stride the needs of three teachers with their brood of two dozen children who range from five to six years of age. I am asked to join the group in a picnic shelter for a supper of barbecued bratwurst on a bun and then, for the adults only, barbecued steak on a slice of bread. It is a relaxed gathering, with the hostel couple doing the barbecuing and tending to the condiments, the children lost in bits of conversation and the teachers resolving the odd minor issue.

From this lofty perch, we get a spectacular view of trees, meadows and towns in the distance. Big bales of hay line nearby fields, but I've seen few farm animals. Our host explains in German that the hay from this area is shipped to parts of Italy that can't grow enough hay for their farms' needs.

After supper the children play games outside, and I get a close look at a series of wooden panels on the lawn. These describe the glacial activity that created the numerous hills, and they show where distant communities are located. The town of Coburg is indicated beyond a series of hills, and I try to ignore the fact that they will need to be tackled on my way to Coburg tomorrow. My information shows no hostel in that town, so I'll need to find a hotel there.

The evening becomes chilly, with nothing to stop the wind from whipping across this hilltop. The hosteller suggests I have a bottle of beer, so I sit alone in the dining area, huddled over my bottle and hoping to warm up before I go to bed.

For the first time on my European trek, the pillowcase has a zipper. That means little, but it's another tidbit to keep me amused in my daily grind. We are provided cozy coverlets, and – by 7:30 pm – I'm huddled under mine to keep warm. On my treks, I live in an artificial environment as I move alone through town and country. Then I briefly meet tourists and staff at hostels or eateries, and I appreciate the kindness they show me as does the amicable group at this hostel in Schnett.

Friday, June 9, 2017

At the hostel's breakfast table, I meet two interesting young people. I ask Daniel about his job, and he responds: "I consult with companies to provide information technology support for their security." I'm not sure what that entails, but it sounds impressive. I saw Daniel arrive on his motorbike yesterday, and he explains: "I'm riding through East Germany alone for a holiday. Old political borders are often kept the most natural, so I'm exploring nature in the area where old East and West Germany met."

Also at breakfast is Juliana who stopped here on her way to a soccer game somewhere. She mentions: "A few years ago, I hiked the Spanish Camino from Burgos to Santiago de Compostela. I found out that a long hike can make your senses sharper. Somewhere along that pilgrimage route, I sniffed a bar of soap for sale in a store, and now I can still smell it." I've had similar experiences and know what she means. The three of us finish our breakfast and wish each other *"Tschüss"* (goodbye) as we continue on our separate paths.

Although Schnett is so small that it refuses to appear on some German maps, it's been my haven and heaven – if ever so briefly. I don't want to leave the peace of this hostel but have 42 kilometres to hike to Coburg today, and I head back down the endless slope. After I cut through the community and descend even further, hills rise above me so I'm cut off from Internet service. My path is confusing within those peaks, and I guess at the way with compass at the ready. At some point, the twisted road leads me northward when I'm supposed to be headed south. I hesitate but decide to continue in hope that the road will eventually twist southward again. Thankfully, my GPS reconnects, but I feel despondent over the extra kilometres I'll be doing around all those hills today.

Hiking through pastureland, I come across two men coaxing a flock of hundreds of sheep and a few goats across the road. The young man is dressed in T-shirt and jeans while the older man has a jacket with sash holding a row of emblems decorating his chest. Cars need to be patient as they wait for the German *bäh* and *mäh* sounds (equivalent to the English "baa' and "meh"!) to leap the ditches and scamper into the next field. Meanwhile the older shepherd gives a call of, "Glup, glup, glup, glup," to the bundles of wool kept in check by eight little dogs yapping at their heels. I would have given the two men Canada pins, but the sight of those dogs was successful in keeping me at bay as well.

Here the road's white stripes are not painted but, rather, stuck down with a backing of foil. The odd bit of glittering foil has broken off and lies exposed as a decoration in the tar. Further along, a car overtakes and passes another right beside me, nudging me into the ditch. A theme continues – one I have encountered since my early Portugal hike – as cars wait till they are right beside me to catch up to each other and pass at high speed, just to keep me from getting too smug.

Now, 10 kilometres past Schnett, siding on the houses is a mix of slate, asbestos, stucco and brick in muted colours – cream, gray and black. Church bells ring in the distance as they have so often throughout Germany, giving this mix of fields and woods a pleasant charm.

I may now be passing the groves of spruce trees I saw from the hilltop at the Schnett hostel. As happens so often in my hikes through hilly terrain, I come around a curve in the road with high hopes: I trust that the road will not continue upward but will, instead, head downward to give me a break from my climbing. Sometimes the road goes up, at other times it goes down, but it is always a surprise.

In a small town, most of the houses have cream-coloured stucco finishes, and a man is sweeping his driveway with a machine that looks like a lawn mower with brushes. I stop at an eatery and enjoy *grüner Tee* (green tea), *Zwiebelsuppe* (onion soup) and an open-face *Strammer Max* (a slice of bread fried in butter and covered with sliced ham and a fried egg).

Further along I pass the window of a convenience store sporting an advertisement for *"Lotto Bayern"* (Bavarian lottery). From that tidbit of information, I conclude that I have entered Bavaria, the southernmost state of Germany. I check my map and gather I left former East Germany and re-entered former West Germany (and the state of Bavaria) yesterday, a few kilometres before Neustadt.

I do not see large fields of crops here; rather, there are small pastures and hayfields between the woods. Then, within an hour of leaving forested area, I find myself between rolling farms within a mix of coniferous and deciduous trees that rise above the fields. Then a row of deciduous trees curves back and forth on the banks of a stream, which flows through a meadow. I delight in this calm image when a car zooms past, and I exclaim: "Hey. It's a road, not a racetrack!"

As I enter the town of Coburg, I pass a Burger King restaurant and decide to give it a chance to be as welcoming as McDonald's has been. I order a chili cheese dog as takeout so I can eat it while I hike, but it is not available since they are all out of wieners. I grumble as I leave minus my chili cheese dog: "That wouldn't happen at a McDonald's."

Across from Burger King stands a group of concrete-and-glass office buildings sporting the sign: "Huk-Coburg." These structures house an insurance provider – one of the largest in Germany. Huk-Coburg seems to be a keystone of the community: the name shows up everywhere.

The entrance to Coburg seemed so modern, but the centre is downtrodden, and the place is disappointing as there is no Hostelling International facility here. Throughout Europe I have been surprised at the number of times a small community has many services and a large community has few. Now, here in Coburg – with its population of over 40,000 – there is not a hostel to be found.

I search for an inexpensive hotel and ask a passerby for advice. He had come from England but knows the community well, and he points me in the direction of an old building on a side street. I ring the buzzer, and a man's voice answers following which a key grates in the lock, and the door opens to a woman who says the man is busy. She'll look after me, but I have to talk to the man by phone to negotiate a price, and in the end I have a basic room and a basic breakfast. The experience is memorable; the hotel, forgettable.

Saturday, June 10, 2017

Last evening's sky was a roiling pink and gave us rain through the night, cooling things off for a full day's hike. As I leave Coburg, I pass through the town square where stalls are set up with items like meat, cheese and vegetables – but, mainly, bedding plants. I ask a woman selling flowers for direction to the *Apotheke* (pharmacy) as I need another tube of sunscreen.

After a chat with the pharmacist, I head out of town, passing a series of mansions at the south end of Coburg. Then I need to detour around a construction zone: a rail line is being placed beside the old track, and this takes me on a half-kilometre detour through overgrown pathways. Beside the old discoloured gravel and dirty rails, the new bed and tracks look clean and bright.

This seems to be an area for birds to gather, and I see many varieties as I continue southward. The sky is overcast, but bits of blue are starting to show between the clouds. I'm now coming across more bike paths than I'd seen in old East Germany.

The few people passing on bicycles may well think I'm out for a stroll of a day or two – for a total of fifty kilometres, for example. On their speeding bikes, they can do that distance in a few hours. If they see their route as a long one and mine as short, they are mistaken. I'm not just out for a walk in the country! In fact, to keep conversations from grinding to a halt, I've stopped saying, "I'm hiking through Europe," and started saying, "I'm crossing Germany." People find that more understandable, and it allows them to react instead of being overwhelmed.

I pass small fields with hay gathered in windrows and see few crops in this area. My trail leads me beside a creek where the birdsong is musical, and I wonder if it is part of nesting behaviour. On a quiet road, I come across a number of marshy areas and enjoy this touch of nature as a change from traffic and farms. This subdued setting pulls my mind into fifth gear – the point on this trip where I can enter a dream state of sorts while my body marches automatically.

Near the towns I see small farms with groves of deciduous trees along the road; behind those woods, crops rise on the hillsides. Here in the country, there is farmland, but I notice few houses: people seem to come from town to grow their crops. In a few areas, the hay lies in windrows and is taken from the field as "loose" hay, rather than being compacted into bales. I hadn't seen this for a half-century or more, whether in Europe or Canada.

Each morning I need to make a series of turns to get from the hostel to the main road out of town. In the afternoon I do this in reverse as I leave a main road and make a series of turns to the hostel. Throughout the day there are other intersections as I go from one road to another. In those stretches where there are many turns to be made – going left, right or straight ahead at corners – I dare not take my eyes off the GPS screen as I can quickly find myself on the wrong path.

Today's walk is an exception to all those turns as my iPhone shows I can hike straight ahead along Burgenstrasse for 27 kilometres before I need to turn at a roundabout. This is so unusual that I even take a screenshot of the map showing "27 km." The previous record had been set two weeks ago as a 26-kilometre trail heading straight to the town of Uelzen.

Now this walk becomes an endless bike path up and down rolling hillsides, and I look forward to a break from the continuous hike. I see the community of Kaltenbrunn to my right just off the main road, so I follow a side street into town. Through a hedge I catch a glimpse of a boisterous crowd, whom I assume to be gathered as a family reunion.

I turn the corner toward the entrance to this park where, to my surprise, I see a throng of hikers who have set aside their daypacks and are rubbing their bare feet. Always on my own, I suddenly have a whole contingent of peers. Here about 100 men and women of all ages are gathered on lawns and benches to rest and to enjoy the cranberry cake that is for sale in a booth. One of the men explains: "We're a group of pilgrims who hike 50 kilometres on a Saturday each spring. We hiked 25 kilometres to the church here by the park, and after lunch we walk back to the starting point."

I buy a piece of cranberry cake and take a look inside the church with its complex gold frames around sacred images. I decide that these folks – with their one-day pilgrimage, religious purpose and unending chattiness – are not my peers after all. I feel torn between belonging here and, yet, not fitting into this group, so I hurry on my way.

Back on the bike path, a line of about 50 cyclists head toward me and pass without a word. I move out of the way to give them room and wonder if that is a sign of my subservience in the hierarchy of car, bike, hiker. I'm glad to be on my own with no need to keep up with other cyclists, for example, and no sense of this being a competitive activity. If it were, I would quit. I slow down to scribble a few thoughts in my notebook and realize how easy that is for me. If I were on a bicycle, I would have to stop and dismount. Although my hike is gruelling, it is a simple process that can be easily interrupted.

I had hoped to reach Bamberg today but decide that the 32 kilometres to the community of Rattelsdorf are enough for now. This seems to be a sizable town, so I'm surprised it doesn't appear on my map of Germany. On the outskirts I see a bright, new Italian restaurant and ask for directions to a hotel, as there is no hostel in Rattelsdorf. The waitress (who is the co-owner with her husband) calls into the kitchen and, a few minutes later, an older woman appears. In her dark blue apron, she had been cooking till summoned to translate for me. Apparently, the cook spent a few years in Britain and speaks English with little hesitation. She describes the location of a *Gasthaus* (guesthouse), and I head for it.

The route takes me through a street that lies between walls of stone and looks somewhat like a roofless tunnel. The street is closed to traffic for a community celebration, and it has become a beer garden with busy picnic tables, smoking barbecues and loud vendors at foaming beer taps. I stroll through this celebration and continue down a side street to find the guesthouse.

This family-run business includes a patio café but seems to have aged ungracefully. It looks as though it could use some cleaning and minimizing of shelves piled with trinkets and paper. The adult son checks with his mother who says they have room for me. Then the dour father seems to grumble that I shouldn't have been given a room. The other two ignore his muttering, and the son shows me to my room on the second floor (or "first floor" as they say in Europe, where our "first floor" is their "ground floor").

I return to the Italian restaurant where I sought directions upon my arrival in this community, and there I enjoy a glass of red wine and a delicious plate of spaghetti with meat sauce. Then I stop at the community feast with its beer steins (in two sizes – large and huge!), music and roasted pig, and I order a crepe on a waffle at a booth. Crepe on a waffle sounds odd but tastes fine sprinkled with cinnamon and sugar.

While adults talk and drink, children are entertained on a "bouncy castle," as it is commonly called. I go to bed early with the wail of a rock singer as my lullaby and with surprise at having chanced upon an exceptionally comfortable mattress. The band screams well into the night: obviously, they hadn't walked all day.

Sunday, June 11, 2017

The old couple who are my hosts seemed exhausted and quiet last evening. This morning they are talkative and cheerful as they serve me a basic breakfast while echoes of rock music seem to taunt the stillness. After breakfast I ask my backpack: "Are you ready to go?" It doesn't answer, so I'm still okay.

On my first trek across Europe, I could keep five points in mind till I wrote them in my notebook. Now I'm down to retaining two or three points – others disappear into the mist. Perhaps my older age plays a part in this; perhaps not. I've thought of using a dictating feature on my iPhone, but I'm traditional enough to prefer pen and paper.

A young man is walking his dog, and I approach him for details about the roads leading to the town of Bamberg. While we talk, his dog keeps barking at me. The man seems to think that unusual, but it keeps happening to me. I'm not sure what dogs see in me that is worth all that unwanted attention.

Further on, a middle-aged couple Heidi and Reinhart get off their bikes to chat, and I'm surprised that Heidi knows about my province of New Brunswick. She is the exception, and I learn that she spent a year in our city of Saint John at some point. Reinhart is eager to keep biking, but Heidi is excited about my hikes and spirit of adventure, and she talks about her own experience: "Once a group of friends joined me on a long hike through Germany." I tell her the book about my first trek is available as an eBook on Amazon should she wish to read it.

I mention: "Hostels in Germany don't seem to have a clear purpose. They are trying to serve a lot of different people in a lot of different ways."

Heidi knows some folks who manage hostels and adds: "Right now they're busy trying to figure out how they can best meet the clients' needs. It's been tricky for them."

Heidi and Reinhart are on their way to spend the afternoon in Bamberg and suggest I might see them there. Reinhart briefly joins in to tell me that the town is famous for its beer, and I think to myself: "Isn't that true of every German community?"

Then we continue on our paths toward Bamberg. Later I hear that the local *Rauchbier* (smoke beer) has a distinctive smoky flavour because its recipe includes malted barley dried over an open flame. This brew is said to taste like a cross between beer and bacon – as if a blend of breakfast and beer.

Here in the northern part of Bavaria, the farms seem of poor quality. They scratch out a few hectares between the wild, natural areas. On one farm I see an alfalfa crop planted in rows, which surprises me as I have only ever seen alfalfa as a scattered crop. I pass a field of potatoes where those plants are outnumbered by the weeds. I'm cooled by a slight breeze while, in the distance under a blue sky, I see a healthier field of wheat.

On this sombre Sunday of solitary hiking, I think of my childhood on our farm in Arkona, Ontario. On Sundays our family would be joined by a group of young men who had also immigrated from the Netherlands and needed a home away from home if only for a few hours. Their boisterous card games were so different from my quiet trek. Soon after, a tourist bus with the licence plate showing "NL" (for the Netherlands) passes, and I imagine that group stopping for a Dutch conversation. But on they go.

I understand from my earlier discussion with Heidi and Reinhart that the centre of Bamberg would be an appealing stop for me. However, a visit to that tourist destination would keep me from hiking, so I continue on the road that skirts Bamberg and takes me through a drab commercial/industrial area, which is not the beautiful side of the city. I hope to get to the nicer part of Bavaria – the part I have heard about – because, until now, this state has been a disappointment.

I see a Burger King outlet ahead and stop for a chili cheese dog. However, as was the case in Coburg, the place has run out of wieners, so I leave disappointed once again. I could have ordered something else, but my toughness in hiking can make me unforgiving: if I have to meet high standards, so should others.

I stop at a hotel to ask if they have a restaurant. They do not, but they send me a block away to an expensive buffet, which doesn't interest me; I'd settle for soup and a salad. One of the staff explains: "If you're not choosing the buffet, you have to eat in the bakery at the side of the restaurant."

There I sit with a coffee and croissant while a middle-aged couple nearby engage in a subdued fight. Obviously, they don't want to yell at each other in this quiet public place, but the atmosphere is thick with muttered accusations. I take the only action available to me: I move to the other end of this small eating area and face away from this troubled and troublesome couple.

I leave the café at the edge of Bamberg and pass through a roadside residential neighbourhood into countryside. For a half hour or so, I hike through a tunnel of woods that is next to the highway but with the traffic hidden from view – an eerie sensation where the sight does not mesh with the sound. Entering a town, I catch another unusual sight: a woman scrubs the doorstep of a shop and carries her bucket 20 metres away to pour the dirty water down a storm drain. I've seen this over and over in my European travels and wonder why I don't see this practice in Canada.

It's a pleasant day at 31 degrees and with a slight breeze but a bit hazy with the odd cloud drifting through the heavens. Although on the warm side, the walking is comfortable as the landscape is flat in all directions with not a single hill to climb.

Late in the afternoon, I stop at a village's patio bar for a small glass of beer and ask if they have anything to eat. The university-age waiter brings me a bowl of their only menu item – wiener pieces and bits of raw vegetables in a vinegar/balsamic liquid (tastier than it sounds) while I remove my footwear. Several men at the next table ask questions about my hike, and I surprise them at the distances I travel.

Their reaction tells me that controlled events are never as interesting as uncontrolled ones. They hadn't expected me to arrive in the midst of their Sunday afternoon tradition of going for a drink, and they enjoy this diversion. Then, the waiter stokes my surprise with his own question: "Do you want me to bring you some water so you can wash your feet?" I decline the offer as I need to get on my way, but I muse at his kind words – words that are almost biblical.

Early in this trek, I saw the McDonald's "golden arches" at such a distance that they were barely visible. My yearning for a coffee break sharpened my vision. Now I peer into the distance and see the rounded tops of two trees with a tiny archway on top and realize my subconscious wants to stop at that McDonald's, which is still far off but visible to my pilgrim's eyesight.

After 41 kilometres I arrive in the town of Forchheim to find the hostel closed for a week. This refuge is named for Don Bosco, the saint who cared for people, especially underprivileged children. I'm surprised that his caring followers are not waiting for me with a delicious meal and a comfortable bed – but they're not.

I look for alternative accommodation, and my iPhone leads me to a spot that was the Franken Hotel but has become a restaurant. There my phone runs out of power, and a customer gives me verbal directions to a hotel many blocks away. After a few turns down side streets, I ask a passerby for further instructions and ask someone else a third time. Eventually, I find Stadt Villa Garni where the owner prides himself on the quiet in that part of town. He didn't count on a dog that barks endlessly till nightfall.

After my arrival at the hotel, Joanne and I have a texted "discussion," in which she begins with worry over upcoming terrain: "Just looking at the map and the mountains are coming up fast! Have you thought any more about making it 3 trips instead of 2? Also have you looked to see if there are accommodations within walking distances through the mountains? Do you want me to look?"

Joseph: "I was going to check with hostel staff on the way. They generally have good information. If you want to take a look, that would be helpful too. Today was a good hiking day (though hot) that got miserable at the end. The hostel here was closed for the week. A nearby hotel was no longer in business. I phoned another hotel and, on the way there, my phone ran out of power. I did get here and am ready to crash, as they say."

Joanne: "I just looked, and towns are few and far between! I don't know the distances though! But it doesn't look too positive in the computer here!"

Joseph: "Oh-oh. I'll be challenged, for sure."

Joanne: "Oh dear!"

Monday, June 12, 2017

Frühstück (breakfast) is served at a sister hotel three blocks away. On the way to breakfast, I pass an ornate building that serves as high school, which is silent as the children are home for the two-week *Pfingsten* (Pentecost) period. Then I make a few turns to get to the classy Hotel Plaza where I choose a variety of items from the buffet. I need to stoke the furnace that is my body, and I fill it with a few types of bread and a croissant, meat (including a small liver sausage), a boiled egg, quark, cheese, cereal, mixed fruit, yogurt, two types of juice and coffee. Fulfilled, I return to my hotel to brush teeth, gather things for my journey and leave the key in the unlocked room door as I was instructed last evening.

I pass through the community of Kersbach where a sign indicates the place is another 1000-year-old! Now I'm beginning to see a number of crucifixes, serving as prayer shrines, along country roads. Bavaria seems to be a more

Catholic area than were the predominantly Lutheran communities further north.

The crops are less lush here than they had been kilometres back: the wheat is short; the corn, gaunt. Any land not suited to farm crops becomes industrial development. I see many signs of plants for sale and the odd tree nursery.

I now feel experienced enough with hiking across Europe that I could give lessons. However, I quickly realize that I would have no students as no one would be silly enough to register.

Even the small roads here are busy in the middle of the day, and several times cars insist on passing each other right beside me. Now a car honks in retaliation. I don't mind a short, warning beep if someone needs to turn where I am, but I become annoyed at the long honks of driver irritation. They just have to get used to my presence, though that is impossible as I don't stay long enough in any one place: I quickly leave each community to adjust to the next one. In trying to adapt, I have stopped calling the item on my iPhone "GPS" and call it "navigation" as they do here.

At some point the road cuts through woods for six kilometres of welcome shade. Then the sky begins to cloud over and becomes a mix of blue, white and grey. I cross an overpass beneath which runs a pair of old railway tracks and a new set. I have noticed more freight and passenger trains in Bavaria than I had seen in old East Germany.

The absence of big fields and the presence of trees, marsh and hills continues as I follow small shady roads. These lead into the suburbs of the city of Nuremberg (*Nürnberg* in German) to end today's 35-kilometre hike. I catch sight of the three spires of a church, and each of these is topped with a carved item – a sailboat, a rooster and a dove. This will make a great photo, and I keep hiking till I reach the point where the three steeples balance in my iPhone screen. Then I snap a picture and continue on my way.

The Nuremberg hostel is a grey three-storey stone building with a red tile roof. The roof facing me sports six columns of dormers, with six dormers in each column – so, a total of 72 dormers on this complex roof. This should be an interesting building to spend the next two days, but it is loud with children and has no vacancy. Someone suggests the nearby Burg Hotel on the street named Schildgasse. This hotel proves inexpensive but only has a room for one night. I note in my booklet: "Aw!"

After dropping off my things and taking a shower, I make my way to Burg Hotel Stammhaus on Langasatrasse to book a room for tomorrow evening as I'm taking a day's break from hiking. Then I find a beer garden for some supper and take a walk through this old part of the city. On a hillside of irregular bricks, people are gathered to drink beer from a "self-serve bar." I prefer coffee to beer and hike for almost a kilometre to an *Eiscafé* (ice cream café). There I have a bowl of ice cream with berry sauce and a cup of coffee on a patio while the waiter pays more attention to his cigarette than his clientele.

Over my ice cream and coffee, I reread Joanne's text message from earlier in the day. It concerns the stay of the Canadian folk singer Valdy at our Airbnb during his appearance at the local music venue, Shepody House. In a text message of Thursday, June 1st, Joanne mentioned this upcoming visit, and now she writes: "Just had the most interesting breakfast with Valdy. A well travelled and well read person! Very nice!"

Joseph: "Great!" (Interpretation: "Wish I were home!")

Back at the hotel, I drift into sleep, but voices awake me through the night. Outside my window a conversation among a few men and women continues for hours, it seems. I keep being roused from sleep in the hope they are nearly finished talking. Then I drift off once again.

Tuesday, June 13, 2017

In the morning I go shopping for a booklet at a Lotto convenience store and for contact lens solution at an *Optik* (optician). This is a good reason to traipse all over the old city, which is surrounded by a wall as are so many European city centres. In my wanderings through crooked streets, I get lost a few times but the GPS on my iPhone brings me back to the hotel.

I take the time to cut my toenails, using more care than I would give this procedure at home. On the trail attention to the state of my feet – chafing within the confines of my boots – becomes a priority. Then I pack my things and move to my next home for the night, the Burg Hotel Stammhaus on Langastrasse.

I find the city's central library, a modern structure with the words, *"Stadt bibliothek"* (city library), appearing on the concrete ceiling of the entranceway. There I type my "Trek Message 7" to family and friends back home. Then I locate an outdoor store and a bookstore, but neither of these have information about my planned route into Austria. I'm troubled by the need to deal with all those mountains and keep looking for information that will, hopefully, ease my mind. On that challenging route, my iPhone will need to be in working order at all times, so I find a Saturn electronics store where I purchase a backup battery.

At my new hotel, I empty my backpack and sort through the extra pamphlets, local maps and plastic bags. To my surprise these unnecessary items fill half a garbage can, and I'm relieved to leave this extra burden behind. I convince myself that my clothes are not yet soiled enough to warrant my searching for a laundry facility, so I do a hand wash of T-shirt, socks and underwear in the bathroom sink.

Then I set off for another stroll and, at the hotel doorway, meet an elderly couple from Kitchener, Ontario and enjoy an English conversation. Their taxi arrives, and they continue on their way while I find the hostel where there was no room for me yesterday, so I can take a picture of its roof. Finding just the right spot, I succeed at getting all 36 dormer windows on that half of the roof into a single photo frame.

The city is best known as the location of the Nuremberg Trials, which decided the fate of the top officials of the Nazi Regime after World War Two. For its importance in history, that event has left little evidence unless one seeks it out. In contrast to the horror of those years, the 19-metre-tall *"Schöner Brunnen"* (beautiful fountain) provides an attractive photo. This 14th-century fountain is located in Nuremberg's main market next to the town hall and looks like an ornamental Gothic church spire.

I continue into the fort that served as protection in the medieval period. In its secret garden, I perch on a bench to take in the view of the city below. Adjacent to the fort is a brewery, which serves its own dark beer and a potato salad that is a disappointment with its chunks of potato floating in vinegar

141

and with the odd speck of green. For no known reason, as I sit there, I have one of my rare migraine events, which consists of a shimmering around my field of vision but with no headache or other symptoms. Then that's it, for another year or so. Perhaps my body is telling me to slow down and sleep the day away in preparation for tomorrow, but I still have more to see.

I feel as though my senses are fully awake to take in the taste of the potato salad, the smell of flower blossoms and the sound of the bathroom fan. In fact, through both of my European treks, those fans have made a most annoying sound at a frequency that I find aggravating. The highlight at day's end is a refreshing shower, which is hard to enjoy because the exhaust fan is connected to the light switch and can't be silenced. Now I seek some quiet in the swimming pool and sauna in the hotel basement. This spa is peaceful: I'm its only client, and there's no annoying fan.

Wednesday, June 14, 2017

Last evening it must have been the turn of two men to be outside my window talking into the night. From time to time, their conversation was interrupted by marauding gangs of young people led in chants by a leader. The leader would shout a string of words, which was repeated by the group trailing behind. I closed my window at some point through the night, and at 6:00 am the two men are still talking. I had chosen a smaller room that faced the street because it cost 10 Euros less, but I hadn't been informed that these sound effects were part of the deal.

This hotel is fancy enough to provide a housecoat for guests. I wear mine, just because I can, but it proves to be much too small for my big frame. As with all hotel rooms, this one comes with a television set. Since the start of this trek from northern Denmark, I haven't turned on a TV set a single time. My concentration on the hike doesn't allow for irritating distractions.

The breakfast at this hotel is elaborate. Instead of the normal bread, meat and yogurt, the cook provides cute canapés, complex salads, quiche tarts and deep-fried cauliflower. Once again, I am thankful for the quiet atmosphere since most eating establishments no longer have radios and TV's blaring as they did on my first trek across Europe. That was a common occurrence but has not been my experience on this trip, which proves to be another mystery of travel. Maybe everyone agreed with me and turned off those disruptions at some point in the intervening five years.

On my hike out of the city, I come upon Ehekarussell, a fountain with a ring of statues apparently portraying Hans Sachs' poem "Bitter-sweet Married Life." Among the mythical creatures is a nude couple. Lying back, and with lips nearing, the man and woman gaze into the partner's eyes while their bodies cuddle against each other.

This is the kind of erotic exposure that I don't see in the public works of art in our city of Moncton, New Brunswick, Canada. In matters of prudishness – as with so much else – it is tricky to generalize in comparing Canadian and European standards. As I hiked through those countries, Portugal and Spain seemed to have a sense of public modesty similar to that seen in Canada. However, Denmark and Germany appear more relaxed in their display of nude statues, for example.

A few blocks further along, is a place where Catholics can stand spiritually naked and exposed to the love of an almighty God. This is the *Katholische Pfarrei St. Elisabeth*

143

(Catholic parish of St. Elizabeth) one of the nicest churches I've seen. A dome in simple rectangular patterns of black and brown hovers over the assembly who are gathered in pews angled toward the fluorescent white altar. The only thing I find disconcerting is the presence of 12 apostles, each in a niche, gathered above the community. Other than the stares of these twelve tall men, the church has a peace and reverence I appreciate.

At the edge of the city, the pilgrim symbol of stylized shell in yellow and blue appears, this time on the post of a traffic signal. As I have noticed previously in such cases, there is no other indication that this marks an established pilgrimage trail. Nearby, at the far end of a Burger King parking lot, four miniature cars are marked with company logos and plugged in to prepare for the evening's delivery of fast food. I pass a grocery store that is unusual in its layout since it occupies the ground floor of an Arotel hotel, while the guest rooms occupy the upper two floors.

Out in the country, the canola is now well past its flowering stage, and pods are forming. As I walk along, several surfaces – roads and sidewalks – consist of the uneven stones that irritate the soles of my feet. As my feet have grown more tender over the kilometres, these irregular surfaces have been an irritant on both treks. I've even chosen to hike through ditches to avoid them.

I suddenly have a hankering for a bottle of Coke and stop for one at a service station. While standing at the counter paying the woman for my purchase, I feel something touch the back of my bare leg. I turn to face the owner's big black dog and fly out the door. I slam the door behind me and look through the window at my hiking poles leaning against the counter, my Coke standing on the counter and – behind the counter – a puzzled look on the clerk's face.

The dog lumbers to the back of the store, and I enter quickly, pay for the Coke, ignore the usual platitudes about her friendly dog and grab my hiking poles. My fear of dogs causes me to shake as I stand outside the shop drinking my Coke. Back on the trail, I pass a few camels in a field – part of the circus collection for an upcoming show in Schwabach. At least these animals are minding their own business.

Back in Aalborg, Denmark, I encountered three elephants loafing beside a circus tent, and I've seen numerous signs on roadside posts announcing that the circus was coming to town. In this circus season of thrilling routines, the acrobats make sense, but I've detected a European sensibility around care for animals. When I hiked through the Netherlands, someone mentioned that construction of a road was stopped because a bird's nest was in the way, and the project could continue only when the fledglings left. Often the treatment of animals has been of great concern, so I'm surprised at this control of elephants and camels for human enjoyment.

I stop at a McDonald's and, after a cup of coffee, take a drink from my water bottle. As I push the lid closed with the bottle at an angle, a thin stream squirts a woman in a group a few tables away. She touches her hair and looks up to see if the ceiling is dripping. It is not. I avoid her glance and study my iPhone – and leave in peace.

Later I pick up a few words of a German conversation, and it sounds like, "This is crazy," which I'm sure it is not. I seem to see more than the normal amount of humour in strange occurrences, and I assume my self-talk is a result of my isolation from normal conversation. In any case, I spend a lot of time discussing with myself the unusual things I encounter.

As I begin to sweat in the sunshine, a cyclist passes, and I envy his staying cool in the currents of air he creates. I'm now hiking along a busy two-lane highway, which occasionally sports a welcome few kilometres of bicycle path. Here the tractors look smaller, and the crops look shorter than they had further north.

A 35-kilometre hike brings me to the hostel in Spalt-Wernfels (located in the town of Spalt, but using the Wernfels post address). The man at reception asks for cash, and I have only 60 Euros with me. He finally agrees that I may use my credit card for the total of 89 Euros for bed, dinner and breakfast. This seems excessive, but I'm tired and glad to have a bed for the night. Moments later he informs me that he made a mistake and gives me back 40 Euros. It's a confusing beginning to a pleasant stay.

The hostel is housed in a 13th-century castle with rock-enclosed spaces that serve as children's play areas. An older group of students forms a camp for learning English and is led by two young men – Eric from the state of Georgia in the USA and Nick from Australia. Though they speak a standard English, Eric and Nick's differing accents show through and must be a challenge for their students from time to time.

Eric convinces me this is the perfect job when he explains: "Organizations from all over Germany contact me to hold an English camp somewhere. I get a good salary, and they pay my expenses. I just show up to tutor another group of young people through play activities and films." I'm sure Eric doesn't do this work for the meals: the supper is grim in its choice of wieners with potato salad or fried tomatoes with cheese. The dessert choice of watermelon or canned peaches is the highlight.

One of the students complains to Eric because another boy is making their room messy. Eric explains: "Nick and I need to be supportive, but the students have to sort things about among themselves. We need to follow some procedures, but we shouldn't be too strict." It looks like Eric and Nick have found a good balance in dealing with their brood of youngsters.

Just before midnight I'm awakened by a party in town, with the thumping, thrumming bass beats making their way up into the castle. I leave my upstairs room in a cottage within the castle walls and walk toward the sound to see the celebration lit up in the distance. Then I have trouble finding my way around the castle's abutments and through its shadows back to my room. I'm just pleased that this isn't 400 years ago when the castle sentry would have been suspicious and threatened me with his spear.

Thursday, June 15, 2017

I start the morning with a little joke: "I think I'll go for a walk today!" And so, I do.

In this part of Bavaria each driveway is a bed of irregular stone. On a long hike, the slightest unevenness can trip me up, and these bumpy patches become a repetitive hazard as they cross the sidewalks. I need to remain on guard since a twisted ankle could end my hike.

Today is *Fronleichnam* (the Feast of Corpus Christi) here in Bavaria. On the one hand, I appreciate the feast day shrines in front of people's homes, the blue and white flags fluttering from the buildings and the ancient costumes for a procession of banners out of the church and into the community. On the other hand, I'm frustrated in experiencing yet another holiday when I'll find most services closed. Here in the community of Grossweingarten, the collection of children watching the parade address the elderly as "Opa" and "Oma" (German and Dutch for "grandpa" and "grandma"). This tugs at my heart as Joanne and I are given those titles by our own grandchildren back home.

I enter an active area of cherry orchards, grape vines and fields of oats and hay. Stopping at a café, bright with its large windows, I have the biggest strawberry sundae I've ever seen. Several groups of friends meet there for coffee, cake and celebration. As I leave the restaurant, I'm pleased to see that stores and other services are opening, now that the church service and processions have concluded.

In the community of Stirn, a celebration is starting in the municipal park. People are gathering at picnic tables and on benches under tree branches and umbrellas. A "bouncy castle" – sponsored by Allianz, a European financial services company – stands inflated for the onslaught of local youngsters.

At the entrance to the community of Pleinfeld, a sign mentions three Catholic weekend Masses and only one Protestant Sunday service. This is the opposite of the ratio I saw further north in Germany where Protestantism has a much stronger presence. I stop at a fancy restaurant in Pleinfeld and have a bowl of a mushroom concoction with two slices of spiced bread dipped into it. It proves to be delicious, and I follow that up with a tasty salad with a flower on top – all of that accompanied by a beer to quench my thirst.

A poster advertises the upcoming concert by the music group, "The Sweet," and I assume this must be a revival of the group from the 1970's. They were a British glam rock band,

and I had enjoyed their hits, such as "Fox on the Run," "Ballroom Blitz" and "Little Willy." It would be fun to stick around and watch this performance, but I have kilometres to go.

As the day progresses, the temperature rises to 34 degrees with a 39% humidity. Three times over, my T-shirt is soaked with sweat and then dries to a level of dampness. I continue to be concerned that, under those conditions and the strain of a continuous hike, water is not enough to maintain my electrolyte balance. Then I add juice, Coke and coffee from whichever establishment is open. In a gas station, I purchase a bottle of Mezza Mix, which seems to be a combination of Coca-Cola and an orange flavouring. I'm fussy about mixing flavours, and this combination proves disappointing.

Here in the country, chapels appear as roadside shrines with seating for a half dozen people and a religious image or two. I stop at one of these to sit and study my map, which indicates it's another 15 kilometres to the next town of Eichstatt. That's too far away for me to arrive today, and I begin to worry about finding a bed for the night. I enter an area of continuous forest and watch for signs of huts in the woods. These simple dwellings are available in parts of Germany for hikers to seek refuge for the night. I don't see any huts and fear I may have to nestle into the underbrush for an overnight stay.

A car comes out of a side road in this wooded area, and I ask the middle-aged couple: "Where could I find a place to stay before Eichstatt?"

They suggest: "Go back seven kilometres to the town of Weissenburg, toward Bayern. You'll find a hotel there." They are definite in their claim that nothing is available out here in the country, but I refuse to turn back though it's now late afternoon. On the trail I live in constant hope that something will show up, that things will work out.

A few kilometres on, I crest a hill and see a building with the word *"Gasthof"* (guesthouse) emblazoned in big letters. I become hopeful, only to have my hopes dashed. This place was once a guesthouse but became a café where about 30 young people are having pizza on its patio. The kitchen staff are busy but helpful in discussing among themselves and then translating into English. They advise me, "There's a country hotel about five kilometres from here in Schernfeld," which happens to be the direction I'm headed, going southward.

Close to an hour later, there is no sign of this accommodation, and I stop at a farm where a family is sitting in a side yard enjoying a barbecue supper. Much to my surprise – and relief – these folks are from France, and I feel comfortable enough with their language to have a conversation. In my booklet I write: "My French words fell over each other in joy!" The family assures me that I'll find my hotel a kilometre or so down the road.

Finally, I see a sign in the distance and turn left to enter a beautiful rustic country inn. The elderly man at reception is welcoming, and the price for a room is one of the lowest I've encountered in German hotels. This place serves people who want to take a break from their busy routine in its park-like setting.

As it's late in the day, the man at reception suggests, "Go for supper right away before our restaurant closes," so I postpone my shower. Now, an hour after being stuck with no home for the night, I'm enjoying *Spargelsuppe* (asparagus soup) and a beer as I overlook a manicured grassy area – with children at play – leading to woods beyond.

The restaurant patio serves as beer garden with its stained wooden beams and picnic tables. Some of these tables are also lined up on the lawn. At one of those, a family with an adult son in a wheelchair is caught up in having a good time. They look beyond his awkward movements and stuttering speech, and they see a son and brother. I'm reminded of that park in the city of Szczecin, Poland and another wheelchair with a young man whose father wiped the drool from around his mouth. As recounted in my book, "Europe, One Step at a Time," I was struck with insight into the cause of my trek during that incident in the park: "I have searched my head for a reason and find it in my heart." Now in a park-like setting 700 kilometres south of the one in Poland, I'm reminded where the motive for my hike lies – not in my head, but in my heart.

The day finishes with a WhatsApp conversation with Joanne: "Lots of hills today, and 34 degrees at some point!!! Maybe Austria will be cooler."

Joanne: "Higher in the hills may be cooler. How many days to Austria do you think?"

Joseph: "Not sure yet how many. I try to avoid thinking too far ahead. Perhaps a week."

After this 41-kilometre hike to the community of Schernfeld, I fall into bed exhausted. At 11:30 I awaken to a cacophony of pelting rain and clattering thunder, with streaks of lightning showing off.

Friday, June 16, 2017

At breakfast my place setting is indicated by a folded card with the script, *"Herr Koot"* (Mr. Koot). I'm impressed. A few tables over, a middle-aged couple are absorbed in a Dutch conversation. I'm tempted to say, *"Goedemorgen,"* and practise my mother tongue. However, they appear to be lost in their own world, so I think better of it. Later, as I leave this paradise and hike to the road, they are headed into one of several trails on the property, and I'm tempted to have a Dutch chat, but – again – I let them be in peace.

Yesterday, on the feast of *Fronleichnam*, I saw many people out on bicycles and motorbikes. Today those folks seem to be back at work because I have much of the route to myself. For a few kilometres, my hike follows a bike path down into a valley and continues between trees full of birdsong. It is an easy walk and leads to a McDonald's for coffee. Sometimes these things work out well. Now the road veers toward large fields: these turn out to be massive crops of oats, a harvest I've rarely seen on this trek.

As I enter the town of Eichstatt, following the hiking route suggested on my GPS, a man waves and shouts from a distance. I stop as he bikes toward me and gives me advice in a mix of German and English. Apparently, the route I am following becomes a busy highway, and he suggests: "Take that street. It is not *gefährlich*" (dangerous). I follow his suggested route down side streets that take me back into countryside.

Today I'm hiking 32 kilometres to the city of Ingolstadt. To maintain the rhythm of my hike or to fight boredom, my brain produces nonsense verse. The latest such jingle incorporates the upcoming cities of Ingolstadt and Munich (*München* in German): "Ingolstadt, Mun-uchen; Ingolstadt, Mun-uchen; Ingolstadt, Mun-uchen; Ingol-Ingolstadt." I keep this up till I start to climb the fourth set of serious hills I've encountered in Germany.

I've seen many signs promoting candidates for an upcoming election. As a visitor, I can ignore all these and not have to make a decision that can follow me into the voting booth. I also decide to ignore the route suggested by my GPS as it doesn't direct me down a bike path where a sign shows that path headed toward Ingolstadt. The trail I choose leads me through a 10-kilometre forest of pine and deciduous trees and past piles of logs. Then farm country starts again – with fields of wheat and oats – and I'm delivered right into Ingolstadt.

An hour ago I realized I'd be arriving at the hostel later than I would like. This anxiety gnaws at me on many afternoons – worrying that the hostel staff have gone home by the time I arrive. As it is, the manager is still in the reception area, and she charges the reasonable price of 21,60 Euros for my night's stay.

Meanwhile I keep getting further behind as the hosteller leads me to my room, and I try to get my stiff hiking legs to keep up. After a day's march, they have trouble climbing stairs and turning corners. Settled in my room, I unpack and take a well-deserved shower.

Some of my toes are mysteriously forming dry skin layers, which cause no discomfort and then peel off. My big toes look as though someone beat them up: the nail beds are black with congealed blood, and the cuticles are worn. The odd blister comes and goes.

Various physical changes appear with each hike, and this time I had the scorched areas on my ears as a distraction. These originated in that Wolfsburg barbershop, and the char has finally disappeared while the hair is already growing back.

And, as usual on these hikes, I'm thinner now. I ponder the effect this hike has on me. The hike should provide a balance between pleasure and pain. And I think of other alliterations that need to be kept even – discoveries/dreariness, excitement/exhaustion and freedom/frustration. As long as these keep balancing, I should be okay.

As it turns out, I'm early enough to have supper with the other guests, a group of college students from Russia. They are returning to the hostel from their local practicum in farm economics – from what I understand. The robust woman serving as cook, in her dark outfit and white apron, calls each of this boisterous group, "Kowalsky."

I ask the motherly receptionist: "Where can I do my laundry?" She responds that she'll do it for me for a small fee as she gives me a basket for my clothes. I bring her the basket and then stroll along a few blocks near the hostel. I'm cold in my T-shirt and shorts while my warmer clothes are being washed, so I take a look at a monstrous church in the old town and head back to the hostel.

By bedtime my clothes haven't been returned to me, but through the night the basket with items – dry and folded – appears in my room. I share the room with Andreas who is here to visit with friends among this loud group of Russian placement students. Andreas left to go to a party with those chums right after supper. In the middle of the night, he hasn't returned, so it must have been a successful party.

Saturday, June 17, 2017

As I hike out of Ingolstadt, it strikes me as a tired-looking city with little renovation among its old structures. I ask a woman the name of the wide river flowing through the city, and she says, "Don't know," and I think she must be a visitor. A moment later I realize she said, *"Donau,"* which is German for "Danube."

On most Saturday mornings, I come across a market as I hike out of a town, but here the streets are quiet. In this city the bike and pedestrian sections of the sidewalks are clearly separated – sometimes with a short hedge between the two. Now I'm surprised, on this early Saturday, to see a young man pass on a unicycle.

As I leave Ingolstadt, I get confused over the route to take. A new bridge has been built, and the road in front of me does not agree with that on my GPS map. I stand there hesitating – picturing where the bridge on my GPS information would have been located and deciding how to proceed – when a pedestrian approaches. He came from the grocery store, and I ask him for help. He motions toward the bridge as the only way to continue southward.

Then he asks where I'm headed, and I tell him, "Salzburg," and he almost drops his grocery bags in surprise. He can't imagine that, on foot, I'm aiming for a place almost two hundred kilometres away.

Then he adds, "But Salzburg is that way," as he beckons southeastward. He isn't considering that the river, a railway track and the Autobahn lie in my way, so I need to follow a road that allows me to cross each of these.

I cross the bridge and successfully continue on my way when a man gets off his bicycle to say hello. When I ask his advice on my route, he says: "I can't help you with finding the best path. I always bike through this area, and biking and hiking are so different. I have to stay on smooth trails on my bicycle." In both of my treks across Europe, people have often been less than helpful as they suggested directions that were –

in fact – not suited to hiking. These may have led me to major highways or twisting paths that added to my day's kilometres. Now I've discovered someone who knows that hikers are unique.

Ingolstadt seemed to be a rundown city that could use renovations, but a lovely walk beyond that city tells me I've left it behind. I now enjoy a series of pleasant features, as scribbled in my notebook: "Villages, horses, crops, grapevines, potato fields in bloom, woods, breeze, big clouds, chapels, churches." Then come a list of other tidbits, as mentioned in my notes: "Friendly people, vegetable juice, freight/passenger trains, highway, few dogs, corn, wheat, benches, people walking in woods and bird chirps."

At a store I discover a few juices to try: the tomato-vegetable mix is tasty; the red-beet juice, less so. The latter concoction is sweetened to the point of its having to decide whether it is a vegetable juice or beet-flavoured nectar. That just doesn't work.

I'm repeatedly reminded of two features of this area – beer gardens and church bells. Beer gardens are located everywhere, and church bells chime throughout the day. Tradition supports the fact that beer is the drink of choice; history supports the fact that Catholicism is the religion of choice.

The odd car license plate now includes a different initial, such as "CZ" or "RO." The former make sense, since Czechoslovakia is the country immediately adjacent to southern Germany and northeast of here. The latter is harder to explain since Romania is several countries over to the east of this spot. Of course, my time can now be taken up with musing about this, and I wonder if this Romanian car is here on a holiday or belongs to someone working far from home. In any case, such queries remind me that I'm actually getting somewhere on this snail-like hike through Europe.

During my 41 kilometres to the community of Au in der Hallertau for the night, I realize that the climbing plants I thought were grapevines are actually producing hops. The plants coil up vertical strings that are attached to horizontal wires three metres overhead. Hops are used in beer production – of course, because this part of Germany is all about making, selling and drinking beer. After the first few, I see dozens of such fields and can't help but think the beer culture is overstated. I'd suggest socializing over mugs of hot chocolate instead.

A few kilometres later, I again realize that my fear of bridges and overpasses has diminished from my panic during the first trek across Europe. Now I can stand on an overpass – though not too close to the railing! – and watch as traffic zooms under me while I dare myself to take a picture of the scene.

As I saw on my hike through Germany five years ago, tall wooden poles are a common feature for the month of May. Although it is now June, many parks and public areas still sport a community maypole, and each is different. Some are simple structures with a few decorative features while others have coloured material winding down the pole's length, as well as horizontal dowels from which little banners wave. In any case, I have not seen any ceremonies around the maypoles: unfortunately, I've missed those community celebrations.

Over the course of this trek, I've visited many churches – Protestant and Catholic, large and small, simple and ornate. Here in Bavaria the mainstream religion is Catholicism, and many of their churches have *Zwiebeltürme* (onion domes) towering over them as does one in the near distance. Suddenly, a white car passes just as two fawns cross the road. Thank goodness, they miss each other by centimetres.

With their traffic, stoplights and crowds, large cities make hiking challenging. Therefore, I decide to avoid crossing through the metropolis of Munich by heading southeastward as I leave Ingolstadt on my 200-kilometre hike toward the Austrian border at Salzburg. As it turns out, this route provides no hostels, and I send Joanne a text message: "I ran out of hostels, so I'm trying a different approach. I'm heading directly for Salzburg, Austria and staying in hotels on the way. Then a day off there – probably Thursday."

In Au in der Hallertau, I find the Hotel Gasthof Rosenwirt and register in its bar. A number of men around a table are chatting till I start speaking English to the hotel owner. The men's conversation stops abruptly as all attention turns toward me. After all these kilometres through 11 European countries, I'm used to being the stranger in town. However, my audience normally doesn't make its curiosity so obvious!

After settling in, I go for supper at Onassis Biergarten – a glass of dark beer and risotto with shrimp scampi. And, yes, it is delicious. This is actually my second time at this restaurant: I went there on the way into town in the afternoon to ask the way to the hotel. The young man left the desk to find someone who spoke English. When the second person arrived, I spoke to him in my broken German, and he spoke German back to me. It was a strange moment: I was pleased to speak enough of their language that he continued in it. At the same time, I had the feeling I left the young man at the desk confused about my language ability. Which is okay because I'm confused about it as well.

Sunday, June 18, 2017

Yesterday, when I arrived at the hotel, I was asked: "What time do you want *Frühstück*?"

I responded: "Is 7:00 o'clock okay? I want to get on the trail early." The owner agreed that 7:00 am would work since I was the only client, and now he is the one to serve me breakfast.

Then I get him to take a picture on my iPhone, showing me in front of his hotel as I'm leaving. As a business owner, he made sure to include the name on the front of the hotel in the picture. In fact, in the first photo, his sign is more visible than I am! I ask him to move a little closer for the second picture, and then I'm on my way. I hope his business does well: he seems to have purchased it recently, he works hard at customer service and he has a young family. So, please spend a night at the Hotel Gasthof Rosenwirt in Au in der Hallertau, Bavaria. I'm glad I did.

Other than the walkway, when I leave a hostel or hotel, mine is always a new road – one that nobody could predict. This morning that path takes me past healthy crops of corn, hops and hay. I notice that bicycle routes in Bavaria are more clearly marked than they were in previous states, with distance markers on clear route signs. I pass wayside shrines of chapels and crucifixes as the GPS directions lead me into a path of gravel running between spruce and oak trees. A fawn appears ahead and looks curious but just as quickly disappears. Even on this Sunday morning, traffic seems to be in a rush – as was that deer – and I realize that I am also in a continuous hurry in my aim to get to the next bed for the night.

I think back on the flat landscape in Denmark as I come upon my fifth set of serious German hills. Here even the sidewalks tend to be hilly, and I ponder that I'm again being prepared for the mountains of Austria.

Strangely, today is one of seeing planes – jets, small aircraft and a few helicopters – making their way through the heavens. I'm not sure why they all show up today, but this is the first time I've seen the sky so busy since Aalborg, Denmark.

Meanwhile the cricket chirps dominate the birdsong. On this interesting Sunday, I look for a church to go to Mass, but all I see in a passing village is a cemetery chapel, which is closed. And, in a nearby field, a tractor pulls a new-looking machine making square hay bales. These bales are actually rectangular, but – in my youth on the farm – we always called them "square bales."

I've heard the distant cooing of doves from time to time, and now, in the community of Langenpreising, I stop to record that haunting sound. I'm looking down at my iPhone to access the "photo" feature and switch the setting to "video" when a middle-aged man approaches. I noticed him sitting on a park bench, and now he asks: "Do you need help finding your way?" I assure him I'm not lost, and he suggests the next hotel on my path southward.

I notice that this man is strangely dressed: he's wearing an old-fashioned white shirt with strategic frills, as well as a scarlet velour vest and baggy black pants. His one gold filling glitters as he talks, and I think this must be a local eccentric who dresses up on Sunday afternoons. Then this "dandy" demolishes my assumptions when he mentions: "I'm an actor in a play, and we're practising in the community hall. I'm taking a break until it's my turn on stage."

At that moment I'm reminded not to jump to conclusions about the people I meet. This strange person is simply an actor dressed for his part. Of course, that still doesn't explain the glittering gold tooth. It also doesn't keep me from my biases as, moments later, two young men and a young woman bike past and I muse about one of the men: "He had enough metal in his face to build a fence!"

I have now entered an expanse of farm buildings. Further north in Germany, I noticed that farmers came from town to work their fields. Here the homes are imposing, and they remind me of the houses I saw in the Basque country of northern Spain as I entered that country from France on the Camino de Santiago de Compostela pilgrimage route near the city of Pamplona. In "Europe, One Step at a Time," I explained the history of these homes: "They would have housed livestock on the lower level, people in the second storey and laying hens in the attic." And that may well have been the case in these three-storey homes, but I see no one to ask, and I just keep walking.

I pass under fluffy clouds through a number of hamlets that form the entrance to the community of Taufkirchen with its 6000 inhabitants. Previously Bavaria was disappointing with its noisy industrial plants and disregard for nature. Now the scenery has become a pleasant combination of farms, hills and churches.

A few times I've taken pictures of colourful cables being placed in the ground. These come in a dozen hues and must be colour coded for technical reasons. However, it's disappointing that stretches of such colour are hidden from our view.

After a 44-kilometre day, I arrive at the classy-looking stucco and wood of Hotel Am Hof in Taufkirchen only to find the door locked. It is late afternoon, and I check at the café next door. The waitress escorts me back to the hotel where she points to a buzzer that alerts the receptionist who gives me a room. I always seem destined to get a room a few floors up, especially in hotels or hostels with no elevator. In this case, I don't have a final hike to my room since it is located just two doors down from the front desk, thank goodness.

As sometimes happens, there are several places called "Taufkirchen," four of which can be found in Bavaria. To distinguish this community from others, it is named "Taufkirchen (Vils)," whereas the others are Taufkirchen (bei München), Taufkirchen (Mühldorf) and Taufkirchen (Rottal-Inn).

Today is Father's Day in Canada, so – in celebration – I feel okay about staying at a higher end hotel. Besides, it's the only one in town, and I'm not ready to hike to the next hotel in a distant town. I receive a text message from Joanne: "I gave the kids your number in case they want to call you or send a message for Father's Day!"

Throughout the day I receive texted greetings from each of our five children, and a final message from Joanne: "Happy Father's Day Joseph!"

Joseph: "Thanks. I'm now in Taufkirchen (Vils). Went to a beer garden to celebrate Father's Day." After stew and a dark beer from a local brewery at *Taufkirchner Biergarten*, I find an *Eiscafé* (ice cream café) for a huge "After Eight" sundae and a cup of coffee to wrap up my solo Father's Day.

I feel exhausted but force myself to do a hand wash. With no heat source or fan in this hotel room, I hang my things in open windows. In the early morning hours, it is cool enough for the room's radiators to warm up and I place my clothes on them in hopes of drying them completely.

Monday, June 19, 2017

The cramping in my legs and feet was bad enough that it kept me awake last night. I took a Motrin tablet to take the edge off the pain. That worked.

At this higher-end Hotel Am Hof, the breakfast consists of a buffet array of dishes made of egg and various other ingredients. It is just too complex to be enjoyed, I think. In fact, the word "yucky" comes to mind, though I still eat enough to keep me going today.

As I leave the hotel, a swarm of conversation passes. It springs from the hundreds of elementary school students walking to their three-storey school. They are returning after the two-week *Pfingsten* (Pentecost) break and, obviously, have a great deal of news to share.

I hike out of Taufkirchen under a clear sky full of expanding vapour trails. The landscape leads me to slow down on the way up rolling hills displaying lavish crops and speed up as I enter valleys clustered with trees. I play with a possible title for my book about this trek: "The Ups and Downs of Europe." Perhaps, "My Ups and Downs through Europe" is catchier.

I recall leaving Europe as the five-year-old youngest of an emigrating family to return in retirement and walk across this continent. I question why more Europeans aren't hiking long distances and decide that such an unusual activity requires an inner freedom, one that came with our immigration. Leaving the Netherlands required willingness to risk starting over and openness to the ways of our adopted country of Canada.

With our immigration came the challenges of combining the old and the new – our Dutch selves and Canadian ways. Our new identities remained more Dutch for older family members and became more Canadian for the younger ones. During this turning point in our family life, I was still a child but received a share of the effects our immigration to Canada had on us. And the adaptable blend that included Dutch and Canadian would be my destiny forever.

The radio hits that were popular in the early 1950's, when we arrived in Canada, are played on the Sunday evening seven to nine o'clock radio program, "Sentimental Journey," with host Loran Fevens. This feature airs on the community station CFTA-FM in the town of Amherst, Nova Scotia and is available in live streaming from CFTA or as a podcast at soundcloud.com. Today is Monday, and I'm disappointed in having missed last evening's program. I look forward to returning home and reconnecting with our Canadian newcomer past of 65 years ago.

Then my mind turns toward two distant churches – one with a spire, the other with a dome. I wonder about the history of these two forms of architecture: "Does God prefer receiving prayers from one over the other?" Through the centuries those churches must have known a lot of prayers. In the sturdy farmhouses of white stucco and red roof tiles, families did what they could to ensure a bountiful harvest, and that included prayer to an almighty God. The houses are plain, not ornamental, and the lack of trees along the road results in little birdsong. All energy has gone into farming and not into complex landscaping or decoration. A rare refinement is the aroma of a U-pick strawberry field enveloping me.

Other than the odd car racing against time, it is a quiet morning. As I hike a road's edge, each of thousands of vehicles requires my undivided attention: I need to watch that it has nothing protruding that might hit me; I need to ensure it passes me safely. Then I concentrate on the next car. A few dead birds and moles on the shoulder of the road have not survived the passing death traps, but I have to survive.

By midday the dome above me is a clear blue with the hint of a crescent moon and with vapour trails hugging the horizon in front of me. The sun is intense as it feeds the many solar panels – on farm roofs and as solar farms – that I have come across over the past week. A stiff breeze picks up, and I'm grateful that it helps cool me under the radiant sun. It also keeps some of the irritating insects at bay although they still succeed in making a meal of my calves. I stop at a highway sign that seems to be whistling a tune as the wind passes the metal sheet and the posts that serve as its supports.

As I enter the community of Ednühle, I notice an arrow pointing to my right toward a bar where I might get something to eat and drink. A woman on a tractor approaches from my right, and I call up to her: "Is the bar open now?"

In another of those coincidences of which I've had many, she replies: "I'm the one who looks after the bar, and it will open late this afternoon. I can't open it now because I have to go and work on the hay in our field." My route takes me to the left, out of town and past the field where I see her on the tractor with hay fluffing up behind it in preparation for its being stored for winter.

I must be getting bored again, as I have come up with a new song to accompany the rhythm of my hiking. This one comes from the GPS instructions on my iPhone: "Take a left on Söllerstadt; take a left on Söllerstadt; take a left on Söllerstadt, on Söller-Söllerstadt." I take a selfie-video of me singing that "song" while I hike, and it will serve as witness to the effect this trek has on me. I'll have to swallow my embarrassment in showing this video clip to others – it's that peculiar!

Strangely, each town in the past 100 kilometres or so has had one crane working at a construction project. I haven't seen two or three cranes in a town – always just one. It's as if the whole region is sharing the few cranes that are available, and the towns get one each. Now I pass a project of threading high-tension power lines onto new transmission towers, and two men are hooked high on those steel lattice structures as they do their work. I know I'd rather hike across Europe than do their job.

As I walk out of the community of Heldenstein, I see mountains rise in the distance and give an audible: "Oh, no!" I assume that's Austria ahead of me, warning me of a tough trail ahead.

At the end of a 31-kilometre day, I arrive in the town of Waldkraiburg and stop at a McDonald's outlet for a coffee and for information on lodging in this community. One of the women at the counter knows of the Hubertusstuben guesthouse, and I head toward it. Her instructions are a bit unclear, and it takes some searching to find the small side street, but I finally get to my bed for the night.

The owner and cook, Vladimir, speaks little English, but he tells his story by pointing to a series of photographs and newspaper clippings on the café wall. These mementos outline his pilgrimages – from Portugal to Santiago de Compostela in Spain; from Lourdes, France to Santiago; from southern France on the main Camino route to Santiago. I have found a true comrade – one who shares the need to respond to the call of the trail.

I sit on the backyard patio for a small beer and supper. That proves to be a pleasant way to unwind. My room provides no heat source to dry my clothes, so I simply decide to leave them dirty and to do a double load tomorrow evening.

Tuesday, June 20, 2017

For some reason, my sleep has been disturbed lately, but last night was a little more restful despite the voices outside my window until midnight. On this trek more people have been lost in nighttime conversations outside my windows than I experienced on my hike from Portugal to Estonia. The reason for this change is another riddle with no obvious answer.

In the morning I enjoy the breakfast Vladimir prepared for the few guests. Then on my way out, he wishes me: "Bon camino!" I appreciate the traditional pilgrimage greeting, which I heard so often in Spain. It has been an enjoyable visit to Vlaidimir's guesthouse and its reminders of my trail eight years – and thousands of kilometres – ago.

As I enter the countryside, I am entertained by a series of implausible sights. So many farm buildings surround me that, from one rounded hilltop, I count 27 farms. I see my first crop of soybeans of this trip but notice that any exposed soil near the road appears parched while I am soaked in sweat as I mount yet another hill. Here the mail is not delivered on foot or by car but in tiny minivans or by bicycle. I hike beside the Inn

Canal and cross a bridge over the Inn River, and I feel uncomfortable about the grey-green fluorescent hue of the water in this tributary of the Danube.

In the community of Engelsberg, a woman is preparing her café for the arrival of the lunch crowd. When I enquire about a meal, she tells me: "My *Essbereich* [eating area] is not ready yet."

So, I ask: "Do you know of a place where I could have lunch?"

In response, she shrugs, and I recognize this as another example of a habit I've seen throughout Europe – the apparent unwillingness of businesses to support the competition. Around the corner I find a large Edeka grocery store, and there I feast on items from their delicatessen area – potato salad and chunks of herring – and wash it down with tomato juice and a yogurt drink. And I think: "*Schmeckt gut!*" (Tastes good!)

The afternoon brings more hot weather, and the sun beats against my face. It is 31 degrees with the humidity at 39%, and I feel vulnerable despite my brimmed hat and sunscreen. My thirst is more overwhelming than it has ever been on this hike, and I take frequent swigs from my water bottle. I stop at a house for a refill, and the woman takes my bottles inside and returns them filled to the brim. I am grateful as a shortage of water can be critical. Back on the trail, I engage in some giddy talk about the lack of electrolytes in water: "Electrolytes, electric lights; electric lights, Edison; Edison, Eddy's son; Eddy's son, Loblaw's son Bob; Bobloblaw." And I giggle.

Finally, it feels as though the intense heat might break thanks to a shower in midafternoon. However, it lasts just long enough to make me put on my rain poncho – which causes me to sweat even more – and take it off again. As soon as the rain stops, it evaporates from the roadway. I feel as though I have not perspired as much in my life as I have in the past week.

I hike into Taching am See, which is a community with a collection of houses and one small hotel in which only the restaurant is open for the start of the season. I stop there to ask the kitchen staff: "Do you know where I can get a bed for the night?"

They suggest: "You can probably find something in Waging am See. It's four kilometres away."

I come to realize that I put the wrong destination into my GPS system, and now I'm trying to find a bed in Taching am See after a 42-kilometre hike when I should have gone the few kilometres further to the community of Waging am See.

This is an example of the challenge I can face at the end of a day's hike: my mind feels a bit muddled, my body presses me to rest for the night and I'm unsure of what lies ahead. In attempting to get better information, I stop at a recreation hall where a woman at the desk points to a few houses on the hill across a valley from their building and says one of those is a bed and breakfast.

I take the road across and looping uphill to arrive in the area the woman had indicated. However, I see no signs for a bed and breakfast, so I stop at a house in the neighbourhood. A couple, about my age, answer the door and tell me: "That place isn't a bed and breakfast anymore." The woman speaks English while her husband does not, but he offers to drive me to a hotel in Waging am See. That's a kind gesture, but momentarily I hesitate over accepting a ride when I need to walk every step. In a split second, I decide that the offer is too good to pass up. Furthermore, I can return the few kilometres to my stopping point in Taching am See tomorrow morning when I continue my hike.

I follow the man as he limps to his car (a knee problem, he explains in gestures), and I pile in with my stuff. I now come to find out that Waging am See is a lakeside tourist mecca with a series of hotels and guesthouses. The first hotel has no vacancy, but the second one gives me shelter for the night, and I thank the man profusely and give him a few Canada lapel pins for him, his wife and their grandchildren.

I send Joanne a text message: "I'm now in Waging am See, a day's walk from Salzburg!"

Joanne: "Oh I loved Salzburg! Are you in the mountains now? As bad as you thought? Good thing you are at your strongest. Thinking of you on the mtns!"

An email message indicates that I have just received the first payment for my eBooks on Amazon, having sold two of them. Then a shower starts, and it turns into a barrage of rain storming against the windows. I close the shutters to keep out the racket and to catch a night's sleep after my 47-kilometre hike (and five-kilometre drive) to Waging am See.

Wednesday, June 21, 2017

At the hotel's breakfast, I am surrounded by 24 police officers attending a training program. They must have overslept as they rush through their breakfasts. And – unlike me – they don't even need to hike to the city of Salzburg today.

It poured rain through the night, but the day turns warm as I leave the hotel to hike back to a spot where I had walked yesterday afternoon. I don't want to miss any distance – even a few kilometres – in my hike southward.

At times I've had to return to a previous point in my hike, and this time, again, it is confusing. Things look so much different when you are heading in one direction rather than the other. Things also seem dissimilar when you are tired at the end of a day's hike or refreshed in the early morning. Making my way along a road and then a path through some woods, I arrive at the recreation hall in Taching am See where I asked for directions yesterday. Having reached my previous hiking point, I can now put my energy into covering the kilometres.

I stop at a friendly *Apotheke* (pharmacy) for adhesive bandages to cover the blistered areas on my feet. Then I set out into the country where I see no cows but do smell ensilage and notice tractors with equipment spraying manure onto the ground. I assume the cows must be kept in barns beyond some of these groves of trees, and I miss seeing them. I don't miss seeing insects as they try to crawl into the orifices of my face. I call them "corn bugs" because they only appear when I pass a cornfield. And then, for a kilometre or so, I see no birds at all but hear the continuous chirping of crickets.

As has happened in previous tourism areas, I see signs for cafés, which point to eateries off the main road. I'm sure the locations are attractive – perhaps even overlooking a lake – but I don't want to take the time or energy required to hike an extra kilometre or more down a side street for a cup of coffee.

A yellow van of the *Deutsche Post* (German mail service) parks along the street of a built-up area ahead of me. The woman who is driving exits with a handful of envelopes, and I approach her: "Can I take a picture of your van?" Then I ask: "Is there a café here?" I assume that, if anyone would have the answer, she would: delivering mail would lead to knowing the community inside out. She mentions two or three eateries across the road, but all of these are closed for *Mittwoch* (Wednesday), and – once again – I am frustrated at European store hours.

On the ground beside the road is a simple stone memorial that lists a dozen local soldiers who lost their lives fighting for the German Fatherland during the Second World War of the years 1939 to 1945. Our Dutch oral tradition includes the role of Germany's soldiers in controlling our lives during that war. Now, here lies another side of that story.

In northern Germany I often heard an expression that sounded like, "Moin, moin," as people greeted each other. Now in southern Germany, I overhear a greeting that sounds like, "Shirt," or is it, "Thirsty"? And I think: "Yes, I am thirsty, and magically I happen upon a service station for a bottle of juice and a bench in the shade. As I sit and drink and ponder the closed services at *Mittwoch*, I think: "It always seems to be *Mittwoch* here – whether Sunday, Wednesday, holy days, some mornings or some afternoons. No wonder Europeans don't hike across their own continent – it's too hard to get services when they keep closing!"

As I hike up to the bridge that serves as the border into Austria, I walk past the line of vehicles going through a checkpoint as the police wave me on. I take a picture of the entrance into Austria and catch the McDonald's "golden arches" in my iPhone screen, so I head for them. There I stop for a celebration snack of a large McFlurry and a medium coffee, when I usually just order a small one of each.

Via text message I inform Joanne of my latest accomplishment: "Just crossed the border into Austria!"

Joanne: "Yay! Is it beautiful?"

5. Austria

Wednesday, June 21, 2017 (continued)

Crossing the border, I arrive in the city of Salzburg and later – facetiously – write in my notebook: "Then the fun started." The moment I cross that bridge, my Internet access is no longer available. Here I need a SIM card for Austria, so my iPhone is of no help in pointing the way. I follow the main road into Salzburg and decide: "This should bring me downtown." However, this road leads to a major highway. I try to cross guardrails and hike through weeds to get to a suburban street, but two-metre fences keep getting in the way. Any attempts at continuing in this direction frustrate me and I backtrack for a kilometre or two when someone suggests that I head for the river and from there turn toward downtown.

Hoping it's the right direction, I hike along a street that takes me to the Salzburgarena. I walk through the arena's empty parking lot in the direction I need to go and end up behind yet another fence. Briefly, I consider climbing this fence when someone tells me about a shortcut to downtown. However, being caught breaking rules in a foreign country is not a good idea – to say the least – and I backtrack with my feet on the ground.

As I walk in front of the Salzburgarena once again, I am struck by the difference in my feeling now compared to that on my last visit here. Now I'm tired and frustrated; back in 2010 I was excited and fulfilled. On a visit to Salzburg, Joanne and I happened to hear of a concert being given in this complex by the Canadian singer, Leonard Cohen. The music, lyrics and emotion were overwhelming and left a lasting impression as Leonard Cohen sang to each of us about our hurts and joys. Now here am I, seven years later, feeling miserable and alone.

Even though I ask a few more people for directions, I don't ever find the elusive Salzach River that I need to follow to get downtown. However, I do eventually find the hostel, but I'm informed: "This building is used for out-of-town students during the school year. It serves other guests only in the summer." The staff suggest I go to another hostel, and they show me its location on their map.

I walk the half-dozen blocks, but the hostel seems to have disappeared as no one in the neighbourhood knows of its existence. I stop at a classy hotel of the Wyndham Group to ask for their help and briefly consider paying their exorbitant fees for a night's stay. However, my stubbornness comes to the fore: I won't give up as I search for an inexpensive room for the night. The front desk staff let me tap into their Wi-Fi so I can use my iPhone to access details on Salzburg's hostels. And they kindly bring me a bottle of water.

This information leads me – after a kilometre or two – to the lovely treed setting of a Hostelling International facility, which has no vacancy, and to three nearby guesthouses, which are also full. I return to the downtown area and, at long last, find the Hotel Wolf that has a bed for me. This whole process has taken the input of 20 strangers and an extra 10 kilometres of hiking through the city with my backpack for a total of 45 kilometres from Waging am See to this hotel in Salzburg. Getting a SIM card becomes top priority: I need to ensure I have better days ahead. And tomorrow's "day off" is well deserved.

I wake up at midnight to the sound of three teens singing in harmony and an adult telling them to stop. Despite this disruption to my sleep, I enjoy their enthusiasm, and I'm pleased that they ignore the adult as they go on their way. Their voices trail off as they continue into the distance.

Thursday, June 22, 2017

After a hearty hotel breakfast, I stroll to the Salzburg Information Centre, in the middle of the tourist area, to find out where I can get an Austrian SIM card. They suggest: "You can buy it at the post office. Then find another business to help you activate it in the German language." They explain where the post office is located and I leave the tourism centre in hopes that, this time, my SIM-card hunt will go smoothly.

As I leave, a man calls me over as he gets on his bicycle. He says: "I was listening to the tourism staff's information and they weren't very clear about where you can find the post office." He tells me he lives in the area and gives me clearer instructions, for which I am grateful.

I follow his suggestions, find the post office and get a SIM card and directions to a photo shop. That store can activate the card and change the phone language setting to "English." However, after I leave the photo shop, the phone keeps sending a troublesome message: "Could not activate cellular data network – PDP authentication failure."

Since the brand name of the SIM card is "A1," I walk two kilometres to an A1 phone outlet. There a helpful young man named Daniel solves all the difficulties, and I finally have a working phone. Even then there is a proviso: to send me a WhatsApp message, Joanne may, or may not, need to call me at a new number or, possibly, at my Canadian phone number. It's all quite confusing.

As this is the part of town where another hostel is located, I hike an extra two kilometres to that building to obtain a map of Austrian hostels so I'll be better informed in upcoming communities. However, the staff there tell me: "The Hostelling International group in Austria doesn't have a paper map anymore. Now all the information is on line." I have used on-line hostelling information but find the directions on a map clearer over long distances. In any case, this proves to be another frustrating hike.

I take the long stroll back to my hotel and use its computer to send out "Trek Message 8" while a piece by Mozart plays in the background, seeing as this is his birthplace. Then I go back to the photo shop for my ballpoint pen, which I had forgotten there, and find a barbershop. My haircut begins with a wash carried out by an apprentice. She brings me a cup of coffee and a glass of water while I wait my turn to have the woman in charge cut my hair.

The "Christmas in Salzburg" store, with its trays of coloured eggs, little lanterns and artificial trees is overwhelming. Joanne and I had visited this shop in 2010 and found it interesting, especially the sight of hundreds of trays of coloured eggs piled in bins. Then we were tourists; now, as a hiker, I find the whole thing nauseating and leave the store at the end of a five-minute glimpse. Then I join the crowd to take a picture of *"Mozarts Geburtshaus"* (Mozart's birthplace) and find a McDonald's outlet with a backyard set up like a beer garden with picnic tables and a wall of ivy.

Rather than tracking down a laundry facility, I do a hand wash of my things. Then I go down to use the hotel computer, which shows few hostels located on my upcoming trail southward through Austria. I find a café for a late lunch of potato soup and beer, and I drop in at St. Blasius Church, which happens to have a Benediction of the Blessed Sacrament in progress. I have rarely seen this ritual since the Second Vatican Council – whether in Europe or Canada – and the large host in a glittering monstrance displayed on the altar now seems otherworldly. I guess that's the idea.

Friday, June 23, 2017

It was another night of teeming rain, but that has, thankfully, come to an end by morning. My GPS map directs me on a paved bike path along the Salzach River toward the town of Hallein, a dozen kilometres distant. Despite mountains all around me, the path out of Salzburg takes me on a level trail with the river on my left and a continuous grove of trees on my right.

I feel disconnected from community life as I hear construction activity, car traffic and factory machinery on the other side of the screen of trees. I miss catching sight of the city's commotion, but my world is always small in any case, only taking in a view of the immediate surroundings. This miniature hiking world is reflected in my simple hiking life: everything I need I carry on my back, in my mind and on my phone.

Two thirds of the way to Hallein, I stop at a riverside café for apricot cake and a cappuccino. The new owner is using a screwdriver to adjust a shelf in the drink cooler and comes over to chat. He is convinced that tourism will keep increasing: "With our warm weather and lakes, Austria is the new Italy." As I leave, a group of a dozen women bike up to enjoy this escape.

For all my concern about Austria's heights, this is some of the easiest hiking I've done in all of Europe. It's almost boring. I cross a bridge to continue on a dirt path as the river, flowing back toward Salzburg, now lies on my right. Nearby a dam creates a bit of a lake, and there are now more houses around me.

As I near Hallein, the river flows more quickly, and I stop in the town for a hot chocolate with *Schlagsahne* (whipped cream). I take my time in looking at my paper map of Austria and checking the GPS information on my iPhone. I need to ascertain which route to take southward toward the city of Ljubljana, Slovenia. The hope of getting to that point on this trip evaporated days ago. I already have my ticket for the flight home from Ljubljana and will simply walk till I run out of time. I now decide not to hike southward through the town of Bischofshofen but to go southeastward when I get to the town of Golling. That looks like it will take me in the right direction.

Hallein is a busy community of tourist, commercial and industrial activity while the downtown is undergoing a great deal of renovation. Leaving Hallein, I continue on a bike path that – strangely – goes through somebody's house. An addition to that beige stucco abode looks like an attached garage with both ends open and with signage directing bikers and pedestrians through this part of the house. Meanwhile, automobiles pass on the roadway within a metre of the building.

At the end of a 27-kilometre day, I enter the town of Golling where the Café Maier bakery sign includes the words "*Zimmer Pension*" (room, guesthouse). I'm warmly greeted by the staff and taken upstairs to a simple, comfortable room. Then I go down for a bowl of goulash soup on the patio overlooking the street.

I send Joanne a text message: "Can you text me on WhatsApp? I want to make sure it works. I got to Hallein by 1:00 pm so decided to keep going. I'm now in a guesthouse in Golling. It was actually an easy walk today!"

Joanne: "Wow! I can't believe you said it was an easy walk! Good to hear!"

Joseph: "Yes, my WhatsApp does work. Every time I get a new phone number, I need to tell the phone a few things, and I'm not always sure I did it right. Most of today's walk was on a flat trail beside the river that goes through Salzburg. It might have been five degrees cooler, but that would have been the only improvement. And a number of mountains are already behind me!"

At twilight I sit on the balcony of my room and hear big band sounds from a few blocks away. They seem to originate in a building that looks like part of a renovated fortress, and I set out to investigate. The venue is stunning with lights making the grey-stuccoed citadel walls glimmer against the night sky. A ramp serves as bridge from the sidewalk, over a long-forgotten moat and into a modernized building that shows its stone origins throughout. Sure enough, the "Ferry Ilg Big Band" is playing American jazz from early in the last century, and I pay the admission fee and take a seat among the locals. I'm the only attendee dressed in T-shirt, rain jacket and rain pants while others are in their Sunday best, but no one seems to mind.

Saturday, June 24, 2017

Buildings throughout this part of Austria are being adapted to serve as guesthouses for the increasing number of tourists. Both these structures and I have a need to adapt; for me, it means adjusting to unusual foods. After covering so much of Europe, I should have got used to the variety of boiled eggs. However, my breakfast in Golling includes an egg that is underdone, where even the white of the egg is still runny. I set it aside and enjoy the rest of the meal, which is delicious. This dissatisfaction reflects my lack of energy and enthusiasm at this point in my hike. I'll soon be heading back home to Canada – and Joanne's perfectly boiled eggs – and my determination to face obstacles along the way seems to be decreasing.

As I set out on this sunny morning, the hike begins without much effort but becomes more difficult as the day progresses. A shallow mountain stream gurgles over clean rounded rocks on my right as it seeks its goal far behind me. However, the sun continues to be hot even in this alpine setting.

I pass a team of young men who are fire fighters gathered on a bike path as they hold a baton-passing competition. I want to stay and watch, but they ask me to make room to avoid getting trampled. That sounds risky, so I hurry on my way.

The path ends, and now a solid line, near the edge of the road's pavement, provides a route for bikers and hikers. As

I continue through the mountains – some of which have streaks of snow on upper slopes – the air becomes cooler. The sun still beams down as I pass many cars and the odd bike but, still, no fellow hikers. I walk past the few small fields that hug horizontal sections in the mountains, and I appreciate the few peacocks, geese and cows. With my farm background, I recognize in the clear mountain air a tinge of the smell of manure.

Having enjoyed visits to the mountains around the town of Banff, Alberta in Canada, I can't help but see comparisons – clean air, rocks and clouds that scrape the mountaintops. The climbing has been minimal till I pass the community of Scheffau, and there an upward struggle begins on a hill that continues its climb into the distance.

A dozen cars and two tourist buses have stopped in a roadside parking area so people can enjoy a hike down lengthy stairs to the geological formation called Lammerklamm. This is a gorge on the Lammer River that boasts powerful currents, deep canyons and the interplay of light and water. A few tourists are climbing the stairs from the geological formation up to street level as I arrive. They are out of breath and complain of the endless stairs: "My legs are sore." As usual, I avoid using my limited energy on this tourism target. I decide to let the wonder that is Lammerklamm go by.

As I climb three long hills in a row, a farmer is riding a small tractor to fluff up a few acres of hay. I stop at a café, and the owner says she has lemon tea. That would be a nice change from coffee, but I'm disappointed when she brings me a bottle of Nestea.

I ask her: "Do you know where I might find a town with a hotel and bus or train service?" I have a vague fear of being caught in a hamlet with no services when the time comes to head home to Canada.

The woman isn't sure of any such place, but her father arrives with a brochure while I take the last bite of my cheesecake. She must have phoned him to ask for information on nearby lodging, and his brochure lists a resort in Abtenau. It looks expensive, so I'm not sure that will be my target of choice for the night. I thank him for the pamphlet and hike the remaining five kilometres into the town of Abtenau.

After an 18-kilometre day – with much of it uphill – I stand in the middle of Abtenau among a variety of hotels and guesthouses. The Hotel Gasthof Post, with its imposing wooden gables, seems to be calling me, and I enquire about a room for the night. As it turns out, that's a good move as this can be a haven while I ponder my situation, and the manager Margret is knowledgeable and helpful.

For 71 Euros per night, I receive a lovely room with balcony and a view of trees, mountains and sky. I also have use of a hot tub and swimming pool; strangely, these are accessed by pushing an elevator button that doesn't move the carriage but opens its side door to the spa area.

I thought of continuing my hike for another day or two southward to a bigger centre. However, I'm running out of both time and determination, so I'll likely catch the bus or train from here to head toward home.

After a seafood supper at the hotel, I find a nearby bistro for coffee and a bowl of "Mozart" ice cream (with its mix of pistachio and fruit). I conclude that this is the end of my trek since I have only four days left before returning home via the airport in Ljubljana, Slovenia. To avoid the sun in my face, I've decided that the next hike will start in southern Greece and continue northward to Abtenau. I don't want to end up in a remote hamlet with little transportation out, so this seems a good place to stop on this hike and to end on the next one when I come north from Greece.

I've been so tough on this hike – enduring discomfort and struggling through it – but, as I sit with my coffee and ice cream, the loneliness hits and tears begin to flow. I grieve the end of this adventure, but I know I'm done.

At the Hotel Post desk, Margret helps me get information about public transportation out of Abtenau, and I consider leaving on Monday, two days from now. I head down the street for a drink of Williamsville liqueur at an outdoor café while a group of German firemen loudly harmonize on traditional tunes. They may be rehearsing for the concert to take place this evening. Later I look for the outdoor venue where they are to be performing but can't find it, and – as I sit on my private balcony – I hear no concert, but I do hear another group of chanting, roving teens.

I take a look at my iPhone and the series of text messages over the past few hours, starting with my arrival here: "I'm now in Abtenau. The long uphills started today, and I'm gathering info on how to get to Ljubljana for my flight home. So, a shorter hike today."

Joanne: "Nice. Just keep the hikes short for the remainder if you can! Is bus or train available?"

Joseph: "The woman at the Gasthof here got the info. The train leaves from various points each afternoon, so I'll be at one of those on Tuesday and get to Ljubljana at supper time."

Joanne: "Sounds good!"

Joseph: "I'm trying to figure out when and where to catch the train. I might take it tomorrow, meaning that this is the end of this hike."

Joanne: "That's fine Joseph! Have a nice few days of rest!"

Joseph: "I don't want to end up in the middle of nowhere to catch the train now or to come back to on the next hike. Also, I'm thinking to go from south to north next time. That would work better for the weather and keep the sun out of my face. I'd get a one-way ticket to Greece in April (hopefully, using Aeroplan miles). Then I'd hike to Abtenau here and come forever!!!!"

Joanne: "What?! And not come home?!?"

Joseph: "Typo: I meant to say, 'Come home forever,' meaning, 'Stay home forever.'"

Joanne: "Haha! Just checking! Lol"

Sunday, June 25, 2017

At three o'clock in the morning, I awaken and decide to soak my aching feet in the base of the shower. I've been fortunate to have these shallow tubs – with a short pipe as drain plug – available in a number of hotels on my journey. Then at six in the morning, I'm seated on the bed sorting through my toiletries and maps. The ritual of shortening my hiking poles and packing them away confirms the fact that this hike is over. I'm heading home.

I join the crowd of 60 retirees at breakfast – their last meal before heading out on their sleek bus. Continuous groups of them arrive to enjoy this retreat, and I'm envious of the simplicity of their getaway. As the bus pulls away from the hotel entrance, a row of staff stands and waves. One might see this as rank commercialism, but their smiles seem sincere, and I'm convinced that both staying staff and departing guests look forward to the next visit.

I go to the village church to attend the 9:00 am Mass, which is being celebrated in honour of today's Feast of the Sacred Heart of Jesus. My teen years at Sacred Heart Seminary were spent in devotion to the Sacred Heart of Jesus, so this is an eerie return to thoughts of that unending homesickness. Now, at 70 years of age, I find that these shorter periods alone on my hike give me a sense of fulfillment of a dream, not a gnawing teenage wish to be home. They free me to open my mind to deeper reflections.

At Mass the parish choir is well versed in sacred melodies and is recognized for its 40 years of service with signs indicating: *"40 Jahre Volksliedchor Abtenau"* (40 years of folk song choir Abtenau). The church building is cherished by the community, but the ancient mould has parishioners coughing throughout the service. The decorative elements seem overdone: I count 30 statues and 30 sacred images in this old church with its old priest. The altar servers are in white gowns featuring wide red collars trimmed in gold. With little adaptation this could serve as a movie set.

The pews are uncomfortable, and I can't put the kneeler up and out of the way as a fellow worshipper has his feet firmly planted in front of it. I'm at the far end of a pew, and it abuts the wall, so I'm imprisoned here. Others in my pew do not leave for communion, and I decide it would take a lot of "excuse-me's" to get to the centre aisle. I consider climbing over the pews ahead of me to escape but understand that would be considered irreverent. My hikes have included embarrassing moments – like taking my boots and socks off in a restaurant –

since I know it's my only visit to each community. But climbing over church pews to get to communion is beyond the acceptable, even for me.

After Mass, the priest presides at the ceremony of Benediction and Exposition of the Blessed Sacrament. Either his age or the infrequency with which the ritual is performed dooms the priest to be hesitant throughout. It seems an awkward twenty minutes: several times the priest realizes he needs to be doing something else, and hurries as he is the one to keep the liturgy going. Following the various rites, I eavesdrop as a woman from the parish is showing a family from the USA throughout the church. I overhear her explanations and appreciate the respect of the community for this worship space.

I head back to my room to pack my things as I need to move to a different room tomorrow since mine is reserved for other guests. I get comfortable in the overstuffed couch and, with my feet on a chair, have a refreshing nap. Upon awakening I recognize a feeling of loneliness: with the hiking pressure off, I have the energy to miss Joanne and home.

I take short walks to photograph the mountains surrounding the town, and after supper I go back for a look at the empty church with its doors still open. It is, again, full of a gathering as the 7:00 pm Mass has just started. This is a much better experience than I had this morning as the priest is relaxed, I have a pew in which I can move the kneeler – and which I can leave for communion – and there is less pomp and no Benediction.

To continue the relaxed feeling, I sit in a patio café in the town square and enjoy a bowl of "lumberjack" soup (pieces of beef and vegetables, with vermicelli) and a glass of beer. As

I dine, the town square becomes the stage for a polka band gathered under a canopy with the church as backdrop. They take a break as a brief rain shower pelts the awnings. Then they're back at their microphones, but I decide it's my bedtime. My room has a new TV set, but it stays off as – once again – I don't want to break the pensive mood of my trek. Instead, I read the four-page bulletin that the hotel produces each day. My hiking is already well in the past: I don't want to sweat anymore, my hiking poles have been put away and my legs are recuperating.

I send Joanne a text message: "I'm still in Abtenau and will be going to Ljubljana by bus and train tomorrow. It rained buckets here today, so I'm glad I wasn't out there hiking and getting splashed by trucks!!!!! Too bad you're not here for a polka!!" (This was sent with 8 seconds of the band's music.)

Joanne: "Haha!"

Monday, June 26, 2017

When a whole new busload arrives, I know it's time to leave. I say goodbye to Margret, who had been so helpful to me. She mentions: "When you arrive here at the end of next year's hike from Greece, I will arrange a celebration for you." I picture the press coverage, the party and – perhaps – a free room, but that's in the future. Now I catch the bus to the town of Golling where I stayed a few nights ago.

Getting off the bus, I find an outdoor café near the Golling railway station. While I wait for the train to arrive, I have a beer, a bowl of soup and a salad containing chunks of meat. I still have more than an hour to go before the next train, so I stroll the few blocks to the Café Maier guesthouse where I spent this past Friday night. The bakery staff are surprised to see me again, but I feel intrusive in trying to talk about something of significance while they are busy serving customers. These folks are likely not interested in details about my hike, so I'm not sure what to say to them. I'm not used to seeing the same people twice, and I prefer passing through new communities so I don't need to discuss my latest news. I resolve my hesitancy by ordering a mocha ice cream cone and heading back to catch the train.

The downtown Golling area still looks familiar as I stroll back to the station. In European fashion, the train arrives exactly on time. As I board, I'm told: "You have to sit in a red railway car." I go from car to car and realize I have no way of knowing which cars are red on the outside. I decide that opening a window and sticking my head out to look at the colours would draw too much attention when a conductor passes and tells me: "You need to be in the next car." It turns out to be as simple as that.

With the rigors of the hike behind me, and a few days in Ljubljana, Slovenia ahead, I philosophize about my trek. Throughout my life I have not been satisfied by the competition others enjoy: I have not felt rewarded in beating the clock or competing with someone else or – even – with myself. Instead, such rivalry discourages and frustrates me. Rather, I see a part of my late father's character in myself: both of us were given a temperament of just persevering in our own pursuits.

Stark mountains pass my train window, and I get out my iPhone to check for messages from Joanne. And I think of how the iPhone – despite the SIM card challenges – has served me on this trek. I wonder how this gadget would have been useful to Saint Francis of Assisi back in 1214 on his pilgrimage from Italy to the distant corner of Spain that is Santiago de Compostela. And I chuckle.

6. Returning Home

Monday, June 26, 2017 (continued)

With the train's arrival in the city of Ljubljana, nearly all passengers disembark. Daniel, at the A1 phone shop in Salzburg, had said I could continue to use the Austrian A1 SIM card in other European countries. If I simply accessed the "data roaming" feature on my phone, its data and phone minutes would be depleted at the rate that they were in Austria. Now, in Slovenia I test that suggestion in using my iPhone to locate the hostel nearest the train station, and it seems to hold true.

Arriving at the massive Tabor Hostel, I am assigned a bed in a room that is cheap and simple. It has three beds, and there is an extra blanket in my cupboard. As sometimes happens, the men and women guests here share common bathrooms. I leave the room key at the desk, as instructed, and take a stroll through the old – but well-maintained – neighbourhood.

I return to the room and send Joanne a text message: "I'm now at a hostel in Ljubljana. Took the bus from Abtenau to Golling and then the train to Ljubljana. My legs and feet are recovering nicely!!!"

Joanne: "Have a nice rest! Is Ljubljana a big city? Nice there? Are you in a hostel there? I'm going to have to google to see what that place has!!!!"

Tuesday, June 27, 2017

Early in the morning, two friendly young men from Britain arrive to occupy the other beds. They seem exhausted and go right to sleep, so I leave our room with its creaky floors and have a chat with the friendly staff in the reception area. They mention: "This building houses high school students from September to mid-June. Then it becomes Hostelling International's Tabor Hostel each summer, which it did just a few days ago."

The hostel staff provide me with a street map, and I set out to explore the city, walking several kilometres through a variety of neighbourhoods. A distant point seems to be the geographical centre of the city, but it turns out to be the commercial hub – streets busy with vehicles and lined with office buildings. The heart of the city is actually much closer to the hostel, and I return there to find a mix of street cafés, stunning architecture and intricate bridges over the Ljubljanica River.

My first impression of the Slovenian people is positive: they are warm and welcoming with not a car horn blaring. The city looks old and tired, with more than its share of graffiti, but parts of it are being renovated. The number of tourists is staggering, and I measure the stretch of outdoor eateries beside the river by counting footsteps as I walk. The total turns out to be 270 steps – so, a quarter-kilometre continuous row of cafés. And that's only one part of the cobweb of drinking and dining establishments.

I catch the last part of the Mass at the Franciscan Church of the Annunciation and then visit the nearby St. Nicholas' Cathedral, comparing the two building styles. At the former, the red colour of the outer walls and roof is symbolic of the Franciscan monastic order, and its two rows of side chapels would have been used for the daily Masses of the priests of that order. At the latter, the interior is dazzling with its gold trim highlighting a series of life-sized images of saints while its green dome and twin towers are city landmarks.

A young family is standing outside the cathedral, with parents discussing the architecture while the young son finds a challenge in the set of bronze doors. He starts climbing the protrusions, seeing this as a rock-climbing wall. His mother notices this and frowns. When the boy doesn't react, she is aghast and tells him to get down – much to my dismay. His activity seemed a good modern use of the carvings on that ancient entryway.

At a patio restaurant, I stop for a pot of green tea, and there I send Joanne a text message: "I'm staying in Tabor Hostel. It may be the least expensive of my trek – basic, but clean and friendly."

Then I add: "Did a few km through Ljubljana today (but no backpack). I think it's a bit like Prague – that older East European feel – but smaller than Prague and not as gloomy."

Joanne: "So is it mountainous there too?"

Joseph: "From the train, they looked more like hills."

Joanne: "Ok!"

Then Joanne asks what I would like for supper when I get home, and I respond: "It's a long list."

Joanne: "Tell me your list."

Joseph: "Dutch soup, potato salad, *stamppot* [Dutch mix of potatoes and carrots, mashed and served with sausage], stuffed peppers, onion soup"

Joanne: "Mmmmm! Sounds yummy!"

After several cups of green tea, I stroll around the old city centre and watch five men put on a gymnastics show. Then a boat passes on the canal with an orchestra playing a marching tune. In contrast, a man is perched beside the bridge, playing complex rhythms on a set of African drums.

I return to the hostel to get information on the transportation I should take to the airport tomorrow. As it turns out, I have a choice of city bus, shuttle service or taxi. I decide the taxi will be the simplest and least stressful at 5:30 am in a strange city. The two men sharing my room leave for a visit to the city sights. In the evening I get bored at the hostel and go for another walk.

This time I witness a short fireworks display in the distance and the drumming and dancing of a Hare Krishna group on one of the wider bridges. And I'm reminded of one of my fellow novices, an American lad from my seminary days of the mid-1960's in the USA. Quite recently he wrote a letter, which appeared on the Internet and detailed the resignation from his position as director of a church choir. It mentioned his intention to enter a Hare Krishna temple in the American Midwest. I think of the challenges of those chaste novitiate days, and I ponder our varied experiences after leaving that monastic environment of our teen years. Now in Ljubljana, Slovenia, I see a chanting group in colourful robes and with short hair, and I wonder how that peer from 50 years ago is doing in his choice of this path to enlightenment.

Wednesday, June 28, 2017

I'm up at 5:00 am, and – with my two roommates still dozing – the floor seems to creak even more than it did yesterday. My feet and legs are starting to return to normal, and I concentrate on finding the less squeaky spots while I get ready to walk to the cathedral for Mass. At six in the morning, there are about 20 of us in attendance for the first of seven weekday morning Masses at this house of worship.

As I leave the church, I come upon market vendors stocking their stalls in a city park. As I amble along, I'm distracted by water on part of the plaza brickwork. Then I notice a sign in Slovenian and English: "The area with Ljubljana's own weather." This feature is meant to be a community secret, but the thin lines hovering overhead must be tiny hoses that spray water to create this damp microclimate on an otherwise dry plaza.

Back at the hostel, I place my laundry in the washer and chat with my roommates who are preparing to check out before noon. Then I put my clothes in the dryer and decide to take one final stroll in Ljubljana during which I get caught in a storm without my trusty rain poncho. With no one sharing the room, I am free to hang my damp clothes at various angles to dry. By morning they should be ready to pack for the trip home.

My long daily hikes became routine, but that pattern is broken with the trip home. I send Joanne a text message for a minor footwear issue: "I'm now trying to figure out whether I should wear hiking boots or slippers on the plane. It's difficult to fit my boots into the backpack."

Joanne: "Take your slippers in the small pack on the plane and wear your boots. Change on the plane!"

Joseph: "Good idea."

Joanne: "Have a good flight Joseph! See you soon!"

Thursday, June 29, 2017

After a restless night, I arise at 4:45 am to pack my last few things. The taxi was ordered for 5:30, and it arrives on time to take me to the airport. Ljubljana must be a city of thunderstorms: on the way to the airport, the third one in as many days flashes and crashes around us. The storm doesn't interfere with our flights as I go from Ljubljana's cozy airport to Zurich's monstrous one.

At the Zurich airport, a number of procedures conspire against me. Upon leaving the plane, we enter a bus, which takes a while to fill before it proceeds. Then the bus takes us to a building where we wait for a train that takes us to the departure area. I race to my gate and arrive there just as it is about to close. As I enter the plane, I switch from stressed to relaxed to frustrated as I, once again, wait for people to manoeuvre their large suitcases into small compartments.

The stretch to Toronto takes us 12,000 metres over Greenland's snow and ice while passengers take pictures as they "ooh" and "aah" over the stark beauty. We arrive in Toronto on time, and I struggle with the new-fangled machine that scans my passport and customs declaration form. I was told at the Ljubljana airport, "Get your backpack from the belt at the Toronto airport and take it through customs," which has been the procedure on all my trips to Europe.

The staff are having trouble with the suitcase delivery system, so the baggage arrives in spurts. However, an hour later my backpack still has not arrived, and I go to the baggage office. The manager there tells me: "Regulations have changed, so you don't need to take your baggage through customs anymore."

I trust my backpack was, in fact, placed in my plane as I catch the flight to Moncton. At last I arrive in Dorchester Cape – with backpack intact – to appreciate the wonder of being home again.

Tuesday, July 11, 2017

Having been home for almost two weeks, I muse on the challenges of resuming my regular routine. The hike was intensive, and returning to a more normal life takes some adapting. Actions that were automatic before my departure now require thought. Soon enough, I remember which garbage items go in which colour of plastic bag, how to work our induction kitchen range and which lever to use for the car's cruise control. It's all come back to me as Joanne and I return to our pre-trek routines.

As has been the case after each of my hikes, I was constantly famished during the first few days at home. A satisfying supper would be followed by a visit to the fridge to see what else I could tackle. Yet, my belts are still finding notches they haven't used in a few years!

More than a week after arriving home, I half-awaken during the night to shimmering images of a scene in Europe and to an urgency to get somewhere. I drift back to sleep, relaxed in the comforts of home and the convenience of not having to look for a hostel.

I'm grateful for the understanding of people in Europe as I was often the exception. With my wish for shortcuts, I'd ask unusual questions about local roads. Thanks to my backpack, I'd take up space in crowded shops. Owing to my hiking regime, I'd eat more than my share of hostel breakfast food. People seemed to admire my dedication, and their interest gave me a boost when I needed it.

I appreciate Joanne's part in looking after things in my absence and in sending out my trek messages. They resulted in responses, which Joanne forwarded to me from time to time. I was grateful for people's interest in my trek: it told me they were concerned, and it helped focus my writing.

Now that I'm away from the trail, I see differences between my hike from Portugal to Estonia and the more recent one through Denmark and Germany, and into Austria. Mainly, I'd learned how to put all my energy into the hike, which allowed me to travel greater distances. Using the GPS feature on my iPhone, aiming for the next hostel and avoiding distractions – those let me cover more territory, and sheer determination helped as well.

The whole undertaking seemed surreal before I went, while I was hiking and upon my return home. I hope, someday, to understand it. In the meantime I'm organizing my notes in preparation for another book when I finish the last stretch – presumably, next year.

I've begun rereading my account of the first trek and found that the incidents described in that narrative were different from my more recent ones. However, at the end of each trip, I've been left with the same question: "Why did I do all that hiking?"

7. Greece

Monday, March 19, 2018

In deciding on a start date for this hike, I had thought somewhere around mid-March would work. I could hike the more southerly route in Greece northward before the heat of summer and the hordes of tourists arrived. Then it struck me that March 19th is the celebration of the Feast of St. Joseph, my patron saint. That date could mark the beginning of this journey.

Catholic tradition and Bible stories create an interesting mythology around the spouse of the Blessed Virgin Mary who is considered the foster father of Jesus. Joseph would have replaced God the Father in guiding Jesus through childhood while refraining from sexual intimacy with Mary, the mother of Jesus. This has been a difficult saint to imitate as his life was a combination of the mysterious and the unusual. However, that's been part of the fun of having my name – a patron saint whose meagre history must have originated in a scripture writer's pious imagination and reed pen.

Now, here I am gathered with family members at Moncton Airport with mixed feelings about a hike through another chunk of Europe. This time I'll be heading northward from the southernmost point in mainland Greece. During my last hike, in which I headed southward, the glare in my face had been overwhelming. Despite the shade provided by my hat brim, the sun had become my enemy, so I'll now have it behind me.

The unique moments of my travel start immediately on boarding when a man, a few seats over, notices a passport in the seat pocket in front of him. It must have been forgotten by a previous passenger, and the flight is leaving, so it's too late to return this precious item to its owner. And I imagine a mini-drama of someone somewhere desperately searching for this passport, fretting over having to obtain a new one and feeling a sense of relief when a complex system from flight attendant to delivery service returns the lost treasure.

Perversely, "air travel" requires a lot of walking: in Montreal I hike from one end of its airport to the other for my flight to London's Heathrow where more walking awaits. As I board the flight in Montreal, the woman in my row keeps hoping no one will show up to sit in the empty seat between us, giving us more room on the flight across the Atlantic. As people approach our row, she lets out a gasp, thinking they might sit in "our" seat. Her prayers are answered, and we have a roomy flight, much of which takes place while I doze.

Again, I am seated in a dormitory of drooling adults and crying babies, and I think of the seminary dormitory in my teen years. That experience, and all the hostels I've used in my later adulthood, becomes a blur of being one member of a slumbering group. Now this sleeping area should be remarkable as it screeches through the air, but it is actually a dark, boring plane cabin. Things brighten when we fly into the morning, and I awaken to take a picture of a pink and orange sunrise against an inky sky.

Tuesday, March 20, 2018

We land at Heathrow Airport, which has been renovated since my last visit. Now it looks less like a bus terminal as it has become sleek and modern. While we board the flight to Geneva, we are told: "After it taxis for a short distance, the plane will stop because it needs topping up with fuel. You must stay in your seats but do not need to keep your seat belts fastened." In all my travels, this is the first time I've been on a plane that had to stop for more fuel. I trust they'll give us enough so we don't need to walk the last piece. I've done enough hiking on this trip!

We do make it to Geneva airport where I spend valuable time in line at a passport control point. Because of this delay, I have minutes to spare before my next flight. I run toward the departure area as an announcement calls for "Mr. Koot" and tells me the gate is closing – or some such thing. I run up an escalator, turn left at the top and trip over a suitcase someone placed there while he was chatting with an airport staff person. I jump over the tumbling suitcase, and a man with a yellow reflective jacket asks my name and says: "I'm here to take you to your gate." Both the staff and I are happy I made it, and the plane is now free to leave.

On the flight we are served a snack in a reusable (not disposable) white plastic box – a bun with smoked meat, pieces of cheese and a salad of quinoa and couscous. From this height the Swiss Alps appear as miniature mountains covered in icing sugar, and I take a picture of this toy landscape.

At the Athens airport, I ask the information desk for directions to the hostel. They indicate the route on a paper map, which I may keep, and they point in the direction of the subway stop across the road from the air terminal. With some help I find the door that opens to the corridor leading to the train. We continue above ground till we get to the outskirts of the city of Athens and then proceed underground. As it turns out, the airport information people have given me incorrect instructions about the location of the hostel, so the "few blocks" become a walk of a kilometre or more through well-worn neighbourhoods.

Hostel Lozanni (also called Hotel Lozanni) is not of the Hostelling International group and does not seem to meet normal standards. The plumbing is problematic: the tap in my room sprays water in all directions, odd holes appear in the shower floor and you flush the toilet in a hall cubicle by lifting a plastic rod in the open tank because the lever is broken. On the good side, the place is inexpensive, and a Vodaphone shop is located across the street. That shop promptly provides me with a SIM card, phone minutes and the data I need to navigate northward on my hike.

There are several bunk beds in my room, but no one shows up to claim the other beds. I use those surfaces to reorganize my backpack in preparation for the bus trip to my starting point. Well past midnight the party crowd returns and takes a while to settle in their rooms down the hall.

Wednesday, March 21, 2018

Last evening the hostel staff gave me directions to the bus station where I can catch transportation to my starting point for this hike. I wasn't sure of the route they had given me, so this morning I ask the person at the hostel desk for clarification and get a totally different set of instructions.

I find the collection of buses, but this turns out to be the stop for city buses in this part of Athens. I ask one of the drivers how I should get to the inter-city buses, and his bus is headed toward the depot, so he'll take me near that point. I finally arrive at the elusive bus station to wait an hour or so for the 8:30 am bus that will take me to the town of Gythio on the way to the village of Gerolimenas.

As the intercity bus pulls away, I'm glad to be leaving Athens. It felt rundown and sad as though its citizens had given up hope of refreshing their city or – even – of getting its garbage systems under control. It reminded me of Naples but without the interesting characters.

On this trek from Denmark, I've noticed much less American music than I had on previous hikes. Now the bus sound system is playing a pleasant mix of Greek songs, which must be lulling me to sleep as I nap off and on. A few times the driver is frustrated with the cars parked on the street and blocking his path. Then there is honking followed by waiting till a shopper emerges from a store to move the car. From the bus windows, I see continuous hills and the odd mountain crowned in snow.

This transportation from Athens goes as far as Gythio where a few of us transfer to the bus that will take me to my destination of Gerolimenas. This service is obviously a local one as the driver and three passengers near him seem to know each other and engage in a continuous, loud conversation. At a 20-minute stop in the town of Areopoli, I order an espresso at a café while a horde of middle school children gathers to board this vehicle, which serves as their school bus. After a 10-

minute drive, a group of them disembark, and the rest do so a few kilometres later.

We follow the coast southward, and I wonder if this is the road I'll be hiking in a few days. I realize I'm now four-fifths of the way through my two European treks, and I still don't understand my motivation.

Only three of us are left on the bus as we have Gerolimenas as our destination. When we arrive in that village, the elderly couple with strong British accents disembark to walk the half block to a four-star hotel for a holiday. I ask them if they know which is the less expensive hotel, and they point to the Katagounas right in front of the parked bus. In her flowered apron, the owner of this small hotel appears, but she speaks not a word of English, and I speak no Greek. She seems warm but businesslike, and I get a room for two nights.

I chose this spot as the start of my hike since it is near the southernmost point of mainland Greece. Apparently, it gets busy during tourist season, but now it's a quiet place. I go for a walk through the area, and sit on a bench to watch the waves roll in. The wind is driving rollers in this part of the Mediterranean Sea. They are angry against the concrete abutments behind several four-star hotels, but then whisper into the ton of pebbles metres from my lodging. I maintain my sense of humour as I write in my notebook that those may be four-star places across from me, but: "In my hotel, only star is me!"

At the hotel the owner takes me to the kitchen to show some of the food she has available for my supper. Choices are limited as I'm the only guest. We agree that I'll have a supper of lentil soup, three pieces of pickled fish and a few spanakopita slices. I ask about a local drink and end up with a

Sparta beer. Later I write in my notebook: "Tasted like drinking a field of grain."

I go up to my simple, tidy room where the top sheet of the bed comes rolled in a neat bundle. Then I reorganize my backpack from flying to hiking mode – taking out my walking sticks, rearranging maps and filling the hip pack with camera, booklet and pen. My sleep is disturbed by an email message from Joanne that we, unexpectedly, owe a large amount on income tax. Her message ends with: "Yikes!"

Thursday, March 22, 2018

During the night the vigorous wind from the south causes my room door to bang against the jamb, giving me no end of irritation. The family in the room across from me arrived late in the evening, and I don't want to awaken their baby with this clanging. I close the door on a folded piece of paper, which proves to be a temporary fix. Finally I place a chair against the door and manage to doze till 5:30 when I arise for the day.

In the hotel's outdoor café, I have a breakfast of a few more pieces of pickled fish, a boiled egg, toast with honey, coffee and a glass of water. From here I see that the Mediterranean continues to roll past the backs of expensive hotels and onto my pebble beach. Yesterday – using complex gestures – I asked the hotel owner how I could order a taxi to take me to the starting point of my hike early this morning. With gestures on her part, she said she would arrange it for me, and it would pick me up at 8:00 am.

At 7:45 there is a knock at my door, and a young woman introduces herself as Michaela. She tells me the taxi is ready to take me to Cape Tenaro (also known as Cape

Matapan). As it turns out, it's no taxi or Uber but a well-worn, dark blue compact driven by a young woman who works at the hotel from time to time. She is accompanied by her friend Michaela who speaks some English and serves as our hesitant translator.

I have placed a water bottle and a few essentials in a daypack and get into the front seat with my hiking poles beside me. Michaela moves a number of items on the backseat to make room for herself, and we are on our way. The road takes a few twists and turns out of this tourist village, and we pass several guesthouses, which are not yet open for the summer traffic.

The route to Cape Tenaro is not marked, and neither woman seems familiar with the area. Since they are not sure of the road, we stop a few times so they can re-orient themselves. As it turns out, we are now behind a series of hills and out of range of Internet service and the use of GPS. Even here, in this remote location, the two women insist on showing me all the sites as the car slows or stops so they can point at an interesting building in the middle of nowhere. As with so many people on my treks, they can't understand that I just want to get to my starting point and start hiking.

Having twice been lost on side roads and returned to the main road, we finally drive up to a spot where the road ends, and from here we see a sign on a post. The driver walks up to it, and her gestures summon us to join her at the marker. This is the area of Cape Tenaro although the southernmost point of land is a few hundred metres down a stony hill, through a rock-strewn field and around another hill or two.

The two women are eager to get back on the road, and they leave me there. The next human being is likely about 10 kilometres back toward town, so I am alone. The rocky terrain toward the peninsula's tip is doable but could cause a twisted ankle or worse. I decide not to chance it.

I am reminded of the starting point of my first hike in Cabo de São Vicente in southwestern Portugal. There I had intended to begin at the water's edge, touch the sea and cross thousands of kilometres of land heading northeastward. In fact, a security fence around that cape's lighthouse prevented me from reaching the water's edge, and the cliff behind the lighthouse would have been a treacherous climb in any case.

Now in Greece on a final hike, I decide to avoid the danger of a tricky walk toward the southernmost point of land and to respect the lack of Internet service should I need help. I take a few pictures of the scene and a couple of selfies, and then I start the 15-kilometre hike back to Gerolimenas.

It's up to 20 degrees here, and I change into my shorts halfway back. I'll be writing in today's email trek message to family and friends: "This short hike was a summary of so many – some sunshine, then a threat of rain, wind from various directions, barking dogs, my stomach becoming a bit irritated, lots of hills – the usual."

Desolate hills feature a rare tourist guesthouse, but no guests. I understand that this area will become busier in a month or so when the tourist season begins. Now, however, I see only one man who has driven his pick-up truck to do some repairs outside a typical square stone guesthouse with a flat roof.

From time to time I catch a glimpse of the Mediterranean Sea as it rolls onto a bit of shore. I stop to take a picture of such a scene when a well-worn van stops and I'm asked if everything is okay or if I need a ride. The vehicle is tan in colour and has the word "UNØ" painted on its side. The driver, who is about my age, has a German accent to his fluent English. As usual, the short conversation turns to the question of where I'm from, and he mentions: "I enjoyed travelling in Canada when my daughter was an exchange student in Vancouver." I tell him of my trek, and he rumbles on his way.

During this hike I've seen a few dogs, which were all on leashes and all barked at full force. As I enter Gerolimenas once again, I see the several mongrels that freely roam through town but never bark or look aggressive.

When I return to the Katagounas Hotel, a German couple travelling through the area are enjoying a beer on the hotel's patio. I order a cup of tea to settle my queasy stomach and notice that my taxi driver of this morning is doing the hotel's paperwork at a nearby table. She says she's surprised to see me at 1:00 pm; she hadn't expected me till 4:00. Then she asks how old I am, and she guesses 50 or so. My response of 71 astonishes her. (And I realize that southern Greece is a long way to travel for a compliment!)

I go up to my hotel room to type my email "Trek Message 9" to family and friends back home. In preparation for this trip, Joanne bought me a lightweight, portable keyboard, which magically types onto my iPhone using Bluetooth technology. I appreciate this gift as it means I no longer need to find libraries for my typing.

My stomach is taking the odd somersault, and I feel generally uncomfortable. My trek message includes the following: "I feel less of an urgency to finish this thing, and I realize it's cutting into our savings. Compared to that first hike in Portugal, so many kilometres ago, I now have a large group of fans. So, I'm letting you all know that, at 71 years of age, I may decide to go home and abandon this foolish dream. Maybe someone much younger will pursue it instead."

At suppertime I walk a few blocks to see what other restaurants are offering as their evening meal. In a hotel dining room, the half dozen guests and the server are focused on an item on TV. They invite me to join them, but I decline as I don't want to attract attention by pulling their eyes away from the action on the screen. Around the corner I find a restaurant with two young couples and an older man smoking cigarettes while discussing the news that is broadcast on the television up on the wall. I find a table some distance away, and the university-age server – in his practised English – takes my order.

Moments later I am brought a dinner plate with two massive gyros kebabs, a pile of French fries and a cabbage salad. I eat the salad with a little difficulty, but the kebab meat gets stuck in my throat. It just doesn't want to go down, and I'm reminded of the number of times my stomach has become nauseated on my hikes. The French fries are resistant as well, and I think: "If only I could just vomit: that has settled my gut in the past. Usually my stomach issues begin later in my hike and only when I've walked long distances. Today I hiked only 15 kilometres, and it was without my backpack, so I should feel okay." I get a sense of foreboding: if I'm starting my hike feeling so bad, things may not go well.

By the end of my meal, much of the cabbage salad is gone, but the rest of the plate looks as it had when it was served to me. While I pay, the manager comes over and, with the server interpreting, asks: "Was there something wrong with the food. You didn't eat much of it."

I assure him: "It's not the food but my stomach that's the problem." I force a smile, though feeling troubled, and head into the night and back to the hotel for a long – and, I hope, restorative – rest.

Friday, March 23, 2018

After a full night's sleep, I trust breakfast will go down well. However, at 7:00 am I am struggling with a grilled cheese sandwich. I know I need the protein and keep chewing until I've swallowed the whole thing. My stomach does not feel as unhappy with the boiled egg, sliced fruit and coffee.

Saying goodbye to my hostess, I give her a few Canada lapel pins for her part-time staff (the taxi people) and herself. She is puzzled as to how to open the lapel pin, so I attach it to her apron for her. She is thrilled and taps her chest with her right fist as her eyes glisten with tears. Her Greek words of appreciation of me as a guest do not require translation, and I hike into the morning.

I climb a long hill out of town, begin to sweat and change into my shorts. Then the rain begins, and I get out my rain poncho. Two dogs – one white with black spots, the other white with brown spots – escort me. I saw these dogs among the mongrels roaming through Gerolimenas and feel uncomfortable with their presence. My fear of dogs is always ready to make me panic, but these dogs do not understand my English pleas: "You can't come with me. Go home." At no time do they act aggressively: when we pass a snarling dog tied in a yard near the road, my two companions cower as much as I do, and we move along quickly.

At the top of another hill, I am perspiring, and the rain has stopped, so I take off my poncho. At the end of an hour (so about five kilometres), one dog stays behind, but the other refuses to leave. It accompanies me past olive groves, rocks, goats, barking dogs, roadside garbage and the acrid smell of smoke.

Here rocks are formed into walls, monuments and the fences around patches of olive groves and tiny fields where a few goats graze. The roadside trash is the foulest I've encountered over the thousands of kilometres through Europe: it is strewn along the road, piled in bags and collected in overflowing containers. I cannot identify the source of the smoke stench, but it competes with the smell of dog poop and permeates everything including me. My stomach continues to rebel, and I sense that this unpleasant environment makes me feel worse.

On the positive side, passing cars move over for me and they go at a reasonable speed. I pass a driveway where I'm surprised to notice the van I had seen during yesterday's hike. I don't see its owner, but then he comes biking toward me and we have a little chat. He says that he painted "UNØ" (for United Nations Organization, I think) on his van because it was stolen several times. He adds: "Now nobody touches it." I ask about the weather in Greece, and he mentions: "Last summer was hotter than usual. It was often above 40 degrees, so I spent many days in the water."

In a village spread along the road, I stop for a cup of tea at a bakery with gleaming display cases. When I emerge, my dog companion is no longer there. I assume the animal found its way home – the 20 kilometres back to Gerolimenas. From time to time, I come across displays of colourful pottery and other items for sale to tourists. Few people are now visiting, but that should change over the next month or so.

After a 25-kilometre day, I arrive in the town of Areopoli, and check the prices at one of the hotels. It is a modern building and includes a restaurant, but it seems deserted. After I knock on various doors, I see a young woman walking through a sitting area, and she points to a door at its far end. Many of my hosts have had something that is of concern to them, and this receptionist's conversation is all about the doors into the building: "I can't get some doors unlocked, I only have certain keys and the front door is always left wide open when there are guests." I was hoping for a better price than 40 Euros per night and decide to check at another hotel a few blocks away.

I feel exhausted but cross the town square to check at the tourist information kiosk for specifics on the prices and availability of hotel rooms. This can save me having to walk from one hotel to another, and I approach the ice cream stand because the person there covers the services at two side-by-side booths – offering both ice cream and tourism details. It must be break time since no one is present, and one of the local people directs me to a nearby hotel. However, the price there is 45 Euros, so I go back to the first one.

When I get back there, the young woman says: "Unfortunately, we just closed for the night because there are no guests." I must have a pleading look in my eyes because she phones her boss, and I can have a room, "But no breakfast." I don't have enough cash at this point and using my credit card isn't a problem. However, her machine won't behave, and she suggests: "You can pay for your room at the bar across the square. It has the same owner as this hotel, and I work there too. Just come with me."

After paying, I return to the hotel, leave the front door wide open as instructed, and – worn out – I fall into bed for a catch-up nap before looking for a bit of supper. A restaurant two doors away has a sign advertising gyros and other food items, and my stomach does a somersault at memories of my struggles with last evening's inedible hunks of meat. Across the square is a pizza place, and I slowly swallow a large slice of all-dressed pizza despite my stomach's objections.

I am having more and more concerns about this hike: my stomach won't settle down, the hills are gruelling and the wayside garbage is disgusting. I am using our limited retirement finances in fulfilling a dream that is starting to verge on a nightmare. At the end of a brief texted conversation, Joanne stays committed to my hike, "I think you should walk," but I have my doubts.

Saturday, March 24, 2018

I leave Areopoli's downtown area, and my "hiker GPS" takes me down a rocky trail near town. However, a fence has been placed across this path, so I hike back to take the road instead. I follow the "car GPS," which takes me on a curved road, and I end back at the spot near the fence across the trail. This must be the epitome of "going around in circles"!

I reorient myself and continue uphill for a two-hour climb. I happen to walk by a bus stop just as a sprinkle becomes a downpour, and I use that shelter to put on my rain poncho. Bouts of rain lead me to put on, and take off, my poncho three times – much to my chagrin.

On a quiet road far from any towns, I happen upon a restaurant with a bakery. The place is surprisingly busy with people eating, drinking and – in the case of a teenaged boy and girl – caught up in a game of chess. I take off my boots, place my feet on the chair opposite and snooze between sips of tea, which seems to be the only thing that my stomach doesn't reject. I feel somewhat revived and continue on my way while trying to ignore the irritation of my first blister in Greece, one located behind my right big toe.

The last hour of this hike takes me continuously downhill and into the village of Stoupa, today's first sizable community. I find the only hotel open this early in the season, but there is no vacancy as all rooms are taken by people participating in a running competition. The man in reception sends me a kilometre away to "Elena's rooms," as he calls them, and I arrive there at the end of today's 44-kilometre hike.

Elena assigns me a room in the ground-floor wing of a house across from her home. From there I walk across a parking lot to a grocery store for supper and breakfast items. I suddenly have an uncontrollable need to vomit and scurry behind the building so Elena, my hostess, doesn't see me do so. I have little success in finding food that I think might settle my stomach, and I bring up three more times in the evening and once early the next morning. My stomach is telling me to stop this hike, and I wonder how long I can keep going.

Sunday, March 25, 2018

I start the day's hike with eating an orange that, thankfully, stays down. Out in the country, I pass a bus stop sign and lay my backpack on a rock wall across the road from the sign. My stomach still refuses to settle, and I come up with a plan. I'll sit up on the wall beside my backpack for 10 or 15 minutes. If a bus comes by during that time, I'll take it and end my hike. If not, I'll keep going. As it turns out, no bus arrives, and I continue on my way. Less than a half hour later on a downhill, the bus sweeps by, heading in my direction, and I simply keep walking.

Since the start of my European hikes, 11 years and almost 8,000 kilometres ago, I have taken over 1500 pictures. With few exceptions, I have avoided capturing images of the repulsive parts of each community. It wouldn't be right to represent the characteristics of an area through a few of its shortcomings. However, I now decide to make an exception to that practice.

A tractor with cultivator attached looks like it has died at the side of the road. Spread over the tractor and its piece of equipment is an assortment of garbage – greasy rags, plastic bags and containers of various kinds. My lack of food is making me feel giddy, and I see this structure as speaking of the ills of our complex world in contrast to the simple beauty of ancient Greek sculpture.

Strangely, I feel as though this country's repulsive side, with its foul sights and smells, has altered my status as objective observer. Instead, it grabs me and forces me to be part of the community: I'm no longer just a stranger passing through. I stop to take a picture of that tractor and cultivator covered in trash from one end to the other, and I feel justified in doing so.

The town of Kardamyli is in the midst of a community celebration, and there I stop for a cup of tea that I hope will be soothing. From a café window, I see a group of boys and girls (in white shirts and black pants or skirts) mill about as they prepare to join in a parade. Then a band in their uniforms arrives, and a short procession marches through the centre of town and arrives at a park a few blocks away. In that treed area of patio tables, people gather as families to enjoy food and drink while the priest in black cassock and tubular black hat socializes with a few parishioners.

On the way out of town, my GPS information shows two routes to the next community of Kalamata. I need to choose between 38 kilometres by car or 27 kilometres on foot. I choose the shorter of the two, and it shows no mercy in leading me up and down hilly roads to a point where I need to follow a trail through rough country.

This time a black dog appears and leads me along a route that is unclear and consists only of a scattering of rocks. Some of the trail has yellow and blue splotches of paint guiding the way, but a turn to the right is not marked. I continue on till I look back and see the dog pointing its snout down this side trail, which I assume I am to follow. I go back and turn as indicated by the hound as it seems knowledgeable about the area, and I think this dog may be my *"deus ex machina."*

The theatre of Ancient Greece included a plot device that the Romans came to name *"deus ex machina"* (literally, god from a machine). This manoeuvre on stage allowed an unsolvable problem in a story to be resolved unexpectedly. The word *"machina"* refers to the crane that lifted a god over the stage in ancient Greek and Roman drama. Just when things couldn't get worse for the characters in the drama, a god would appear at the end of the crane and resolve the plot situation while surprising the audience or making them laugh.

When I am now at my most desperate, this dog (instead of a god) appears and guides me through a scene of frustration, in the drama of my hike, to a safe conclusion. I wonder: "Are the Ancient Greek gods watching over me in my struggles through their hills? Are the gods that must still occupy this land concerned enough to send me that black dog as my *deus ex machina*?"

The 12-kilometre path of stones is a combination of unevenness threatening to twist an ankle, narrow rock ledges above a 10-metre drop and all of that on a path that leads constantly upward. At one point I shake myself as I fear I may faint for lack of food, and I don't want to collapse all alone among these boulders.

Three hours into this gruelling hike, I meet a dozen people from Switzerland led by a guide from the nearby city of Kalamata. They are headed for a well-known "roofless chapel," which I saw an hour ago and thought unremarkable – just a few deteriorating stone walls. The guide comments that the path has not been well maintained, and I think: "That's an understatement!"

After this 15-kilometre day, I continue into the hamlet of Malta, which doesn't appear on my paper map or on my GPS information. There I look for signs of a guesthouse or hotel with no luck. I stop at the Zapnaia bar for information, and the woman who owns the place makes a few phone calls. She can't find a bed for me, so my option is to continue for another gruelling few hours to Kalamata.

The only food I've been able to keep down today is the orange that I had this morning and the odd cup of tea. Now I order a Coca Cola that I sip slowly as I work at thinking clearly while mesmerized by a man lighting the kindling in the café's fireplace and adding a few chunks of wood. It's cool up here in the mountains, and the fire warms the few customers who are lost in conversation while taking the odd glance toward me.

My brain wonders if I can rest somewhere for a few days and try to continue. My heart – and my stomach – say it's over. I'm sick, I don't have an endless supply of funds and the trek will become no easier as I go along. I feel ill enough that going home becomes a positive, not a negative. It's over, and I ask the woman who owns the place a question that becomes a turning point in my European adventures: "Could you call a taxi for me?" I give each customer a Canada pin and take a final selfie in the bar.

The taxi arrives and takes me on a twisting road into the tourist city of Kalamata. The pangs in my gut bring back a feeling from my teen years – my dread in facing another month away from home at the minor seminary. After each monthly visit, the ride back to Delaware, Ontario would see me sitting in the back seat of the car, overcome with a feeling of nausea as I faced another month of homesickness.

The driver asks if I want a hotel downtown or along the beach, and I want to tell him that my dream just died and nothing else matters. But I say, "By the beach," as the waves could be a distraction for me, and he pulls up to a hotel and waits while I check for availability of a room. This hotel lobby smells of stale cigarette smoke, the staff seem confused over dealing with a customer and they start calling to a hidden voice in the back to come and help. The person I need will be there in two minutes, they say, but I escape back to the cab.

A few doors down, I check at the Ostria Hotel and decide that will be my home (and hospital bed!) for a day or two. I have the feeling the friendly, well-informed staff will be of help in my plans to return home. I settle into my room and take an extra-long shower while I realize how unfair I feel toward Greece. I remind myself of the ease in obtaining a SIM card in Athens, the helpful staff and drivers in Greece's bus system and the power of the sea in Gerolimenas. I remind myself to think positive thoughts.

Then, in place of attempting to have supper, I go to bed and sleep. And sleep. And sleep. At some point I awaken to send Joanne a text message: "I'm coming home. Call me."

Joanne: "I love you and just want you to be happy!"

Joseph: "Me too you!"

Monday, March 26, 2018

My room rate includes an extensive breakfast that seems overdone considering there are only half a dozen of us as guests. Perhaps the kitchen staff are practising for the upcoming tourist season when the place will be buzzing. In any case, all I take is a small bowl of Corn Flakes with milk and a cup of tea.

Yesterday's front desk staff said in broken English that a man with information would be available today. Sure enough, a man of about my age occupies an office in the reception area. He must be there as part of the hotel's tourism services and seems eager to help.

I am intrigued by this man's perfect English, and he explains: "I grew up in Washington, DC and moved to Greece to be with my father after my mother died." I have read that planes now leave from the airport here in Kalamata, but he informs me: "Those are only chartered flights. Sometime in April, at the start of the tourist season, a few regular flights will leave from Kalamata."

I send Nicole at CAA (Canadian Automobile Association) in my home city of Moncton, New Brunswick an email message. In it I ask her to arrange a flight home from

Athens and to let Joanne know the details. To get to Athens, I have the option of taking the bus or sharing a taxi with others. The prices are similar, so I choose the taxi, and the driver has *loukoumades* (Greek donuts) for us. I fear getting sick in his car, so I refuse the treat and settle into its back seat to nap for most of the two and a half hours to Athens.

My condition may have led to this strange dream. My sisters Cathy and Pauline, my brother Bill, my wife Joanne and I are in a rented rowboat, which Bill briskly paddles downhill till it splashes into the water in Moncton, New Brunswick. Thank goodness the imaginary rental agency has written the date incorrectly, so they won't be able to look back at their records to ascertain who did the damage.

I awaken with a feeling of relief that we won't be held responsible. In my haziness, I try to make sense of this dream: perhaps, it's a way of resolving my dismay at not reaching my goal while reassured that I wasn't accountable to anyone. And I think of our family and one of my mother's sayings: *"Heb je je best gedaan? Dan is 't goed."* (Have you done your best? Then it's okay.) I did my best and have nothing to regret.

Through the taxi windshield, I catch the words, "Amber Alert," on an overhead pixel sign and find it interesting that I might see a similar feature on a highway in Canada. The trip requires delivery of one man to a town near Athens, and he is greeted by children and grandchildren while I miss my loved ones dearly. The other man and an envelope are destined for Athens itself, and in the end only I remain and need to be taken to Athens airport.

Joanne contacts me about a flight leaving Athens at 6:30 pm, but it is now four o'clock, and we are still an hour's drive from the airport. After some hesitation – and annoyance from the taxi driver who is waiting for clear instructions on my destination – I tell him, "Just take me to the Hotel Lozanni," which is the place I stayed upon my arrival in Athens a week ago. I decide to stay there overnight and get to the airport for a flight tomorrow.

This time I share a room with a man who was a hospital's head pharmacist in the United States and now covers the night shift at the hostel's front desk. He is full of stories about innovations he made in the control of dangerous drugs and the hospital manager's lack of appreciation, which he says: "Led to my early retirement." As he chats on and on, I'm torn between two things: I need this divergence from feeling miserable while I wish he would be quiet so I could suffer in silence.

I repack in preparation for tomorrow's flight home. Then I take a shower in the quaint shower with the odd holes between its floor tiles. The toilet is now in worse shape, with the flushing mechanism having come apart completely. Then I type "Trek Message 10" to family and friends to let them know I'm on my way back to Canada and home.

JOSEPH KOOT

8. Home to Stay

Tuesday, March 27, 2018

At 3:00 am I am roused by an alarm that turns out to be Joanne's wake-up phone call from across the Atlantic Ocean. It breaks me out of a sound sleep to remind me to get ready for my cab ride to the airport for the flight home to Moncton via Frankfurt and Montreal. Then someone knocks on my door to tell me the taxi has arrived.

I'm surprised at the number of cars and pedestrians in Athens at 3:30 am, and then the gleaming airport is a throbbing mass of staff and passengers. In the midst of this activity, I forget to give an attendant my Aeroplan number and return to her desk to do so. I need those points for future trips, even if my trek is now over.

Because of the shape of my backpack, I need to take it to a drop-off point at the far end of the series of airline counters. Free of that burden, I can now take my time going past the glitzy shopping area with its bright lights, perfumes and cognacs to catch my flight to Frankfurt, Germany. I can't help but compare this bright, clean, modern setting with the dark, dingy, shabby city that is Athens. The differences are remarkable.

223

After we land at the airport in Frankfurt, it provides another set of exercises as we take a long hike up and down stairs to our gates. With its Greek SIM card, my iPhone cannot access the Internet here in Germany, and I can't seem to gain entry to the airport's Wi-Fi so I can contact Joanne.

At my gate an old man is arguing with an Air Canada attendant, and he gets more and more agitated. The issue seems to have to do with his being assigned an aisle seat instead of a window seat, or some such thing. He finally settles down, and we can turn our attention to the less dramatic elements of air travel. As I stand up to join the row of people ready to enter the plane, I drop my boarding card, which a young man immediately picks up and hands to me. I'm grateful for his kindness.

Following our walking exercise through the airport to get to this point, the lifting segment begins – people raising heavy weights above their heads. Suitcases are being hoisted into overhead compartments in which they barely fit. Folks of all ages and sizes are engaged in this activity, one that has irritated me on each of my eight trips to hike through Europe. By now I should be accustomed to standing still with my little daypack while my seat beckons far ahead of me and I'm held up by an unending row of weightlifters. I've still not grown used to it and, probably, never will.

Finally, I'm in my seat and enjoy the cultural variety around me. Across the aisle on my right, a Dutch family of mother and two teen sons are watching movies and sharing bits of conversation in my native tongue as they travel from Munich through Montreal to the Dominican Republic for a holiday. A few rows up on my right a woman in first class sips white wine from a glass goblet while I drink red wine from a plastic cup; she has big headphones while I have little ear buds. Here I am, a Catholic-Dutch-Canadian-Anglophone person surrounded by a diverse group.

Next to me, on my left, a woman's lips are moving as she meditates over a Muslim prayer book. Ahead of me sit two corpulent men wearing black yarmulkes, white shirts and dark trousers; one wears suspenders while the other is in dark vest and rimless glasses. I realize that, as we shoot through the sky, three of us need to share one God among us. This Islamic-Jewish-Catholic God is busy keeping all of us safe. And I wonder if those are the real three persons in one God, rather than the Father, Son and Holy Spirit that I learned about in our Catholic elementary school.

After my elementary school years, the religious influences of our family led me to the minor seminary's high school program. I was a thirteen-year-old intent on becoming a priest at the end of a path of a dozen years. After a seven-year struggle, I left the seminary, realizing I could not last another five years to reach the distant goal of ordination to the priesthood. Life as a pious young man in a community closed to outside influence was suffocating.

The boredom that comes with confinement to this plane cabin leads me to ponder the challenges of my distant youth and of my recent hikes. The seminary experience had similarities to my treks across Europe: I was alone within each community; the journey was a series of hurdles; my determination kept me going.

In my heart, I felt defeated at not finishing the trek to priesthood and the one back from Greece to Austria; in my head, I've learned from those experiences that we simply try and sometimes we don't reach distant objectives. That doesn't mean we've failed; it means we must work at accepting how things turn out. With the struggle we put into achieving our dreams comes the need to deal with both fortune and adversity.

In the seminary I had to show only one God that I was staying pure, and I think of the crowd of old Greek gods – about 170 of them – watching me from behind those hills. How they must have been laughing as I laboured over unending slopes, along trails of rocks and through their desolate land. The mythology of the ancient Greeks was the set of stories about gods, goddesses, heroes and rituals that formed part of their religion. The most popular figures in Greek mythology included gods like Zeus, Poseidon and Apollo; goddesses like Aphrodite, Hera and Athena; titans like Atlas. Traces of that mythology appeared in my English literature studies in high school and at university.

The civilization that was ancient Greece lasted for 1500 years, until AD 600, and flourished from the western end of the Mediterranean Sea to Central Asia. Despite a limited population, Greek culture managed to make progress in many fields of philosophy (Plato and Socrates), poetry (Homer), medicine (Hippocrates), mathematics (Pythagoras and Euclid), art (especially sculpture and architecture) and science (astronomy, including the idea that the earth revolves around the sun). Classical Greek culture influenced ancient Rome, which – subsequently – spread that culture around the Mediterranean basin and throughout Europe. Ancient Greece provided the foundation of modern Western culture and is considered the cradle of Western civilization.

The Greeks left a legacy that touches many aspects of our lives. Their athletic prowess – with nude men as Olympic athletes oiled up for wrestling matches – served as the vision for the present-day Olympic games. A visit to the Louvre museum in Paris, France is rewarded with an extensive display of ancient Greek art, especially sculpture. The wars against foreign armies and between Greek factions, including those of the city-states of Sparta and Athens, were covered in my high school's ancient history course.

As a logophile (lover of words), I appreciate the root of "logophile" as coming from the Greek *logos* meaning, "word" and *philos* meaning, "loving." And I can't help but see Greek retribution in our struggle with the plural form of "phenomenon" and "criterion." The plurals are simply "phenomena" and "criteria," but their Greek roots have been a challenge for many radio news writers tempted to add an "s" to some form of those words.

I consider all of that during my plane ride across the Atlantic Ocean and wonder how it applies to my hike in Greece. In ancient times this part of the Mediterranean region must have had a refined culture to produce efficient systems of government, wonderful works of art and great literature. Now on my hike, I saw a whole other side of Greece – one that seemed dreary, dirty and disorganized – and I wonder what happened. Civilizations and cultures come and go, but I wonder if the Greek people don't consider what they've lost and wish to raise their expectations.

In many ways my hike through Greece was the reverse of my experience elsewhere. Here the hills were the rule with little level hiking; in other countries they were the exception. Here agriculture consisted of a few olive trees; in other countries I had seen lush farm fields. Here rocks were strewn everywhere; in other countries I had seen few stones in farm fields. Much of the farm country that provided me with easier hiking throughout Europe had been part of the old Roman Empire. Eventually the Roman Empire was to become dominant over Greece, but Rome's influence too would come to an end, and signs of its demise are now repeated in the xenophobia rampant in the American Empire.

Rome built Hadrian's Wall at the northern end of *Britannia* to keep out the foreign Picts. Romans practiced a state religion that led to the persecution of the believers of other religions (such as Christianity). Beyond the city of Rome, the rich lived in villas with mercenaries keeping guard. So American attitudes are nothing new, whether the idea of a wall on the Mexican border, religious fundamentalism with discrimination against minority faiths (such as Islam) or cowering in gated communities. And, as with the downfall of all empires, the American one contains the seeds of its own demise: mainstream opinions, political systems and wealth distribution support rich against poor. The 235-year failed experiment that is the American Empire is dwindling thanks to its increasing isolationism, growing debt load of 21 trillion dollars and decreasing respect from other powers. A new Chinese Empire – now building friendships with emerging economies throughout the world – is yearning to be next in dominance.

In my pensive mood on the plane, I ponder the remains of cultures and empires evident during my crossing through the European Union. Each of the 13 countries showed something of a complex past.

In Lagos, Portugal a statue of Prince Henry the Navigator (1394 to 1460) hearkened back to my Grade 4 history book "Pirates and Pathfinders." This sculpture had been erected near the hostel where I stayed overnight on my way to the start of my hike in southwest Portugal. It commemorated the prince of Portugal who used Lagos as a launch pad for many of the expeditions he commissioned. He was responsible for the early development of Portuguese exploration of Western Africa and the islands of the Atlantic Ocean, as well as the search for new trade routes.

In Spain many of the churches on the Camino de Santiago de Compostela pilgrimage routes were adorned with dazzling *retablos* – massive carved panels, often gold-encrusted, adorning the walls behind the altars. For many years Spain had a virtual monopoly on importing gold from Mexico and Peru, helping to make Spain one of the richest and most powerful nations in Europe. From the late 15th century to the early 19th, the Spanish Empire included a huge overseas territory in South and Central America and in the Philippines.

In southwestern France north of Bordeaux, I was told that the birthplace of Samuel de Champlain was only 70 kilometres from a bed and breakfast where I spent the night. Champlain (1567 to 1635) had been a cartographer, explorer and colonial administrator who played a major role in founding the colonies of "New France" in present-day eastern Canada – Acadia, Quebec City and Trois-Rivières. He also explored the Atlantic coastline, the Canadian interior and the Great Lakes region.

In my hike I crossed Belgium between Maastricht, the Netherlands and Fumay, France. I sensed a cross-cultural buzz in the city of Liège where, for example, three senior citizens – appearing to be from three different minority groups – were caught up in a discussion at an outdoor café. This mix of people from elsewhere stems, in part, from Belgian dominance oversees, in which the Belgian colonial empire (1901 to 1962) mainly consisted of the Belgian Congo, which was about 76 times larger than Belgium itself.

During my hike through the Netherlands, I was struck by the amount of maritime activity with freighters plying rivers and canals to transport goods from Europe's interior to the docks of Rotterdam. A woman at whose house I overnighted spoke of the years she and her husband had spent on Europe's waterways delivering goods. Such enterprises have historical roots in the Dutch Empire, which included two companies chartered in the early seventeenth century – the Dutch West India Company and the Dutch East India Company. These trading enterprises held a monopoly on shipping routes: some went westward establishing New Amsterdam (later, to become New York) and sailing around South America through the Strait of Magellan; some went eastward establishing Cape Colony in southern Africa and sailing around Africa past the Cape of Good Hope.

In Germany I hiked through both former West and East – democratic and communist – sections of the country. These entities had come out of the resolution of conflict at the end of the Second World War, which had resulted from the aggressive territorial demands of Nazi Germany whereby it conquered most of Europe by 1940. During the Second World War, Germany was conquered by Allied powers from the west and the Soviet Union from the east. The Nazi regime ended after the defeat of Germany in May 1945, and the country was split into West and East.

In Poland I sensed despondency in the downcast eyes of passing cyclists, which was understandable, given the nation's history. Though established as a state in the year 966, Poland has often been controlled by others in the past century and a half. Starting in 1815 it was grabbed three times, in the Austrian, Prussian and Russian partitions. After its renewed independence in 1918 with the Treaty of Versailles, it was invaded by Germany in 1939 and the Soviet Union after the Second World War and then became a satellite state under Soviet influence.

During the 15th century, Lithuania was a formidable power, which became the largest state in Europe through the conquest of others and union with Poland. On my hike through this country, I could sense Lithuanian pride reflected in its everyday culture based on wood – distinctive yellow wooden houses and public art crafted from wood. However, at the end of the 18th century, the partition of Poland had erased Lithuania from the political map. Afterward, Lithuanians lived under the rule of the Russian Empire until the 20th century with a short interruption as property of Nazi Germany.

Latvia struck me as a humble nation with a history of being used by others as outlined by a couple who had immigrated to Latvia from Canada and at whose home I spent the night. After centuries of Swedish, Polish and Russian rule, the Republic of Latvia was established in 1918 when it declared independence from Russia. This autonomy was interrupted at the outset of World War II with its forcible incorporation into the Soviet Union, followed by occupation by Nazi Germany in 1941 and re-occupation by the Soviets in 1944.

Among the Baltic Countries, Estonia seemed the most technologically advanced during my hike, with people paying parking tickets using their smart phones. However, for centuries Estonia had been a battleground where Denmark, Germany, Russia, Sweden and Poland fought their many wars over controlling the important geographical position of the country as a gateway between West and East. In 1940 the Soviet Union occupied Estonia and illegally annexed the country, Nazi Germany occupied it in 1941 and the Soviet Union reoccupied it in 1944.

My stops at Denmark's Kro hotels let me feel like the guest of a historic Danish king. In the 13th century, King Erik Klipping ruled the unified kingdom of Denmark that had emerged three centuries earlier as the nation in control of the Baltic Sea. This king ordered the establishment of a network of Kro hotels as he had been frustrated with a shortage of good lodging when he travelled through Denmark. Now, 700 years later, I have felt like royalty at Kro hotels as I enjoyed coffee or a meal along with a relaxed break from my hiking.

Through my brief hike in Austria, I already saw enough mountains that I assumed they could have served as a barrier of protection from other powers. Compared to the defeats suffered by Poland, Lithuania, Latvia and Estonia, the Austrian Empire was always independent, having come out of the old Holy Roman Empire in 1808. Then Austria formed a dual monarchy with Hungary to form the Austro-Hungarian Empire in 1867. When this empire collapsed at the end of World War I in 1918, Austria was reduced to the German-speaking areas of the empire and became the First Austrian Republic. In 1938 Austrian-born Adolf Hitler annexed Austria to the German Reich, a move that was supported by the Austrian people.

The foreign control described above came to an end for each of these countries, and they are now independent members of the European Union. On the flight across the Atlantic, my musings about European history result in a few notes in my booklet. I plan to expand on those after my return home.

Looking back, I see my hike as a series of discoveries: I learned about the history and geography of European countries; I came to appreciate the intricacies of people's language and culture; I grasped more fully my own strengths and weaknesses. In fact, much of my enjoyment of the journey came from the chance to learn more about countries, people and myself. Now it is time for a nap in preparation for my arrival in Montreal and the hike through its airport to catch the flight home.

Upon arrival at our local Moncton Airport, I am greeted by family concerned with my health. An irritated stomach doesn't show on the outside, and I tend to downplay my infirmities, in any case. My family is convinced I'm healthy, and we're all relieved that I'm home – home to stay.

Thursday, March 29, 2018

Two days after returning home I send out "Trek Message 11." This is my final note and a chance to provide family and friends with the following thoughts about the end of my trek.

Now I'm back enjoying the peace of Dorchester Cape and not having to hike to my next bed for the night. My tummy is feeling better, and I'm quickly getting back my appetite. My stomach has decided that this was my last European hike.

Although I've tried to avoid seeing my walks as a competition, I have to admit that the process is feeling unfinished. However, life is like that, and I can come to terms with the adventures of the past 10 years as I process the information for a book.

JOSEPH KOOT

I appreciate the many responses to the abrupt halt to my trek. Many people were concerned about my health. I've seen the doctor, and he declared me fit. Something in the exertion of long-distance hiking seems to bother my stomach, as it already did way back in Spain.

Now that it's over, I recognize my hike's purity of purpose: it was my way to keep moving. To put all my energy into this constant motion, I had to avoid wishful thinking. "I should have," "if only," "I wish I had" – these are thoughts I needed to avoid so they didn't lessen my resolve.

After my arrival home, a whole series of activity would take up any energy that was saved by not hiking. Joanne and I planned to put our house on the market, look for an apartment in Sackville and send a truckload of items to an online auction service. Our four-bedroom house and its 29-acre property had been a haven for raising a family. Now it was time to downsize as another step in our retired life together.

How do I now feel about not reaching the goal I had set for myself? Only a few regrets remain, and one of those is the matter of disappointing Margret of the Hotel Post in Abtenau, Austria who had planned an event upon my arrival. This could have meant a celebration with a free room and press coverage at the end of the trek. I felt bad in informing her that it would not be happening, and she wrote back with an understanding, supportive email message.

I had also looked forward to the hike through Croatia along the coast of the Adriatic Sea. I pictured the scenery as a continuous view of the Mediterranean Sea, and I had hoped for some flatter terrain along its shore.

I remind myself not to dwell on any feelings of falling short of my goal when others suggest I must be disappointed in

234

not finishing the trek. I appreciate their kindness, and I know their concerns are meant well. However, I need to accept these as simple statements of support since it is not they who needed to hike all that distance under difficult circumstances. Any sense of disappointment is modified by my relief that it's over.

I do wonder how I would feel if I had completed the whole journey. When I reached the coast of Estonia at the end of my first trek, I felt elated at finishing that 6,000-kilometre hike. This time I've missed out on any such exhilaration. However, life is a set of experiences to be appreciated, and I now value the fact that I tackled almost 8,000 kilometres through Europe. I achieved a great deal in my hiking that was both an inner and outer trek. I didn't see the journey as a competition, and yet, I think I won.

Would I return to Europe to finish the hike? Only with a support vehicle and a pile of money would I consider going back. So, it won't happen.

I'm now free – free from carrying a heavy backpack, wearing my passport under my clothing and tying my hiking boots over and over. I'm no longer pressured to keep moving: on a walk to our shore, I can allow myself to sit and relax. I can take a walk, like the one in Europe – along a road, up and down hills, past trees and fields – but without the pressure of distance, the pain of blisters, the search for a bed. Now I'm not tied down by the demands of the hike, the need to wear a rain poncho or the constant sweat that leaves me hot and cold at the same time.

I can take comfort in mundane activities. At our local grocery store, I'm used to the routine and don't need to worry whether the clerk weighs my vegetables, whether I pack my own groceries and whether I need to pay for a plastic bag.

Being familiar with local businesses, I don't need to be concerned that I'll be confused about procedures at the next store.

Here I know my surroundings well enough that I don't need to look at compass, iPhone or map to check my location. Now I'm either at home in a favorite chair or walking down our country road or driving through a familiar community. I can relax in my retirement while I reminisce about the adventures left behind in Europe.

www.ingramcontent.com/pod-product-compliance
Lightning Source LLC
Chambersburg PA
CBHW060206070426
42447CB00035B/2715